Kristine,

LIFE'S TOO SHORT

FOR A BAD BUSINESS PARTNER

or to eat cauliflower...

Bill [signature]

LIFE'S TOO SHORT

FOR A BAD BUSINESS PARTNER

The guide to ending an unproductive business relationship and moving on

WILLIAM PIERCY

Copyright © 2019 William Piercy
Illustrations by Chris Frishe, Graphic Technique
All Rights Reserved. Published 2019.

ISBN: 978-1-7335645-0-2 - Paperback
eISBN: 978-1-7335645-1-9 - ePub
eISBN: 978-1-7335645-2-6 - Mobi

Library of Congress Control Number: 2019900378

Printed in the United States of America

William Piercy
3475 Piedmont Road
Suite 1100
Atlanta, Georgia 30305

www.williampiercy.com

The contents of this book are for educational purposes and nothing contained herein should be construed as legal advice. The information provided in this book is not a complete analysis of every material fact for any industry, business, or legal situation. Opinions expressed are subject to change without notice. Statements of fact cited have been obtained from sources considered reliable. No representation, however, is made as to the completeness or accuracy of any statement or legal data. This publication may include technical or other inaccuracies or typographical errors. Author assumes no responsibility for errors or omissions in this publication or other documents, which are referenced by or linked to this publication or the related website.

Taking or avoiding legal action requires an in-depth review of all areas of a specific situation in order to provide appropriate advice. Such analysis and review are not possible in a book format, but the principles herein are believed to be foundational in nature and are a starting point for gaining knowledge about specific legal issues related to business dissolution. As with everything in life, there is no one right way to approach any issue or problem. What is effective for one person or entity may not be effective for another in a similar situation. There are always pros and cons to any legal strategy, and a strategy which positively impacts one area of a business will most likely impact other areas. Readers are encouraged to seek legal advice from competent professionals in the legal arena so that the specific details of their situations can be considered as a whole.

This publication is provided 'as is' without warranty of any kind, either expressed or implied, including, but not limited to, the implied warranties of merchantability and fitness for a particular purpose or non-infringement. In no event shall author be liable for any damages whatsoever, including without limitation, special, incidental, indirect, or consequential damages of any kind, whether or not advised of the possibility of damage, and on any theory of liability, arising out of or in connection with the use of information in this publication.

Nothing contained herein is, in any way, a guarantee or assurance that following strategies outlined in this book will create legal success or security, and readers should understand that they are responsible for the actions that they take or do not take as a result of reading this book.

To my wife Dawn, whose support made this work possible, and to my son Mitchell, whose curiosity about the world and confidence in me inspired me to finally put pen to paper.

CONTENTS

INTRODUCTION

Business is all about relationships; relationships with customers, relationships with vendors, relationships with lenders and landlords, and often, relationships with business partners. Without these relationships, business doesn't get done. The creation, care, and feeding of business relationships is vital to long-term success.

Although one person can own, manage, and operate a business, many choose to do so with a partner. At its base, a business partnership involves two or more people joining together in a common enterprise to share the work, the expense, the risk, and the opportunity. A partner may bring capital, experience, or labor. A partner can bring accountability and a set of checks and balances.

Your relationship with your business partner may be structured in a variety of ways. Perhaps there are shareholders, officers, and directors in your corporation. You might be a member or the manager of a limited liability company. Or maybe you own part of a professional corporation, or a general partnership. Each form of business ownership has its nuances, but, for purposes of this book, if you share ownership in a business with others you are effectively partners, with intertwined rights, obligations, opportunities, and risks.

When all owners of a business are invested in its success and working toward a common goal, a business partner can be a force multiplier in the growth and success of the enterprise. But sometimes, disagreements about direction, strategy, or commitment become serious enough to distract from the operations of the business. At worst, these disputes can cripple a business and result in financial ruin. When the relationship between business partners sours, business failure is likely to follow.

Sometimes, business relationships stop being productive and become an impediment to growth and success. A bad business relationship can also take an emotional toll. Owning a business is hard enough. Running that business with a partner who no longer shares your goals, values, or work ethic is a harbinger of failure. If you find yourself nodding in agreement as you read this, it may be time to leave your business partner behind. But how? Just as there is a right way to create a successful business partnership, there's a right way to end one, too. That is what this book is about.

If you find yourself in a bad business relationship, this book is for you. Chances are, you never thought you'd be in this situation. And while the thought of a protracted negotiation or costly court battle seems daunting, sitting by as your partner takes all your work and investment in the company for himself and destroys your reputation in the process is no picnic either.

There are many factors to consider if you plan to split with your business partner. How do you divide assets, liabilities, and inventory? Who gets the business name? Who takes the customers? What do you do about the employees and the office lease? The list is long, but not endless. This book is your guide to navigating the process of splitting with your business partner while covering your tail, capitalizing on your opportunities, and emerging with your retirement fund, your sanity, and your soul intact.

In over twenty years of business litigation practice, with an emphasis on officer, director, and shareholder disputes – basically, corporate divorce – I have helped hundreds of entrepreneurs successfully extricate themselves from business relationships along the spectrum from merely unproductive to downright abominable.

I won't go so far as to say I've seen it all, but I've seen a lot. One client audited the company's books only to discover that his partner was using company funds to install a swimming pool in his back yard. Another discovered when his father passed away and his will was read aloud, that dear old dad had three other children from extra-marital relationships. Dad left equal shares of the company to all of his children; leaving my client in business with half siblings he never knew about. Yet another client, who was part of a successful technology company, went to work one day to find that his partner had moved to Romania, taken control of the business remotely, and was diverting receivables into a new Romanian bank account to which my client had no access. While I hope none of these situations ring true with you, if they do, you're not alone.

Maybe you are angry at a partner whose actions never lived up to his words. Perhaps you are concerned that customers, employees, or vendors are bound to notice the dissension in your company's management team. Competitors would certainly view this as an opportunity to grab additional market share. Anger, frustration, depression, resentment, confusion, and fear are common among entrepreneurs who find themselves in an unproductive business relationship. It's not fun, but it's normal. You want the feelings of hopelessness and despair to end, but you don't know where to begin. This book is the place to start.

CHAPTER 1

Business Relationships are Not Meant to Last Forever

Chances are, you like to win. Your competitive drive may be what led you to go into business for yourself in the first place. You're also probably a team player, recognizing that a group with varying talents working together can create something greater than any individual could accomplish, particularly over the longer term and at scale. Perhaps for these reasons, you joined forces with a business partner. Being a competitive team player is a positive attribute for business success. But, this same superpower can also be your kryptonite, causing you to tough it out with a bad partnership long after the relationship outlives its usefulness.

In many ways, the holy vows of matrimony create a partnership. Marriage certainly contains elements of common enterprise and shared risk. That's what 'for better or for worse' is all about. Marriage is also supposed to last "forever"; the whole 'till death do us part' thing. Although about half of all marriages end in divorce, the "forever" aspiration associated with marriage is so ingrained in our collective psyche that many entrepreneurs come to believe, even if only subconsciously, that their business partnership should also last "forever." This is a troublesome myth. Unlike a marriage, business partnerships are supposed to end. Best case, they end with the partners departing as friends with large bank accounts.

The fact that you are reading this book is perhaps an indication that your business relationship is headed down a rockier path. Maybe it's already fallen off the cliff. One way or another, your partnership is headed to a conclusion. As you read this book, you will be able to better shape that conclusion into the one you want, or at least into one you can live with.

WHY DO BUSINESS PARTNERSHIPS FAIL?

Business partnerships fail for many reasons. Among the most common are the following:

Lack of communication. A free flow of open and honest communication is an essential component of a successful business partnership. When dialogue breaks down, bad things happen. At best, the lack of information leaves the left hand unaware what the right hand is doing. At worst, it leads to conspiracy theories and distrust between the owners of the business. Too often, business partners will go weeks, or even months, without communicating meaningfully about business operations and management issues. If it's been more than a few weeks since you've had a productive conversation with a business partner, it may be time to re-think that relationship.

Lack of transparency. Although related to communication, transparency involves access by all partners to the raw data on which the business is run, things like bank statements, financials, and operational metrics. Assurances from a partner that a segment of the business is operating as it should is one thing. Confirmation with backup data brings an additional layer of comfort. "Trust, but verify" is an old Russian proverb made famous by Ronald Reagan. If it's been months since you've seen a company bank statement and your partner keeps coming up with one excuse after another as to why the statements are unavailable, it's time to act.

No shared vision. To move a ship (even a partnership) forward, it helps if everyone rows in the same direction. If one business partner wants to pursue a highly leveraged model towards exponential growth through franchising while the other wants to maintain tight control over one core location, there are rough seas ahead.

No clear/defined roles. A common aspect of start-up culture is that the founders roll up their sleeves and do whatever needs to be done to get the business up and running. As the company matures, founders typically gravitate toward roles and responsibilities that suit their respective talents and skill sets. When that gravitation does not result in any understood or agreed upon division of labor, it can result in two partners doing the same job (wasted effort), or no one doing the job (a wasted opportunity). Either way, it's no way to run a business.

Failure to stay in your lane. Similarly, when a division of labor is delineated, but one partner consistently performs the role of another partner, or interferes with that partner's work, friction results. I've seen it firsthand.

Bonnie and Clyde were equal partners in a successful towing business, but they didn't tow cars. They got the call when a semi broke down or overturned on the highway. Their tow trucks were huge! Clyde ran the crew and maintained the equipment. Bonnie managed the finances, interfaced with vendors, and administered the retirement and healthcare functions. Basically, he was front office and she was back office.

They had clearly defined roles, but they wouldn't stick to them; that, and they didn't talk.

Bonnie frequently rearranged employee schedules in an effort to keep overtime at a minimum. Yet, she knew nothing about the crew, their skill sets, or their personalities. One employee was dating the ex-wife of another employee before the ink was dry on her divorce settlement. Clyde took pains to keep these employees apart, but Bonnie thought nothing of rearranging the schedule and putting the two men on the same shift.

For his part, Clyde would buy anything new, shinny, and pneumatic for the shop without bothering to ask Bonnie. Bonnie often learned of these purchases only when the invoice or credit card statement arrived. Their interference with each other's roles was steering their business into oncoming traffic. More on Bonnie and Clyde later.

Disparity in contribution. Another common source of frustration between business partners results from the perception by one partner, accurately or otherwise, that he is contributing more—more money, more effort, more hours—to the success of the business than is his partner. If familiarity breeds contempt, inequality of effort births open hostility.

The business outgrows its founders. The skill sets, gumption, drive, vision, and risk taking necessary to get a business up and off the ground are often very different than the skills necessary to keep it flying smoothly above the turbulence. Yet, it can be difficult for a founder to let go and pass the controls to someone else, even when the time comes to do so.

Failure to hire professional help. As businesses grow, they have more sophisticated needs. No entrepreneur, no matter how skilled, can do it all. Wise entrepreneurs recognize this and hire appropriate professionals; lawyers, accountants, consultants, technical support, etc. These professionals help keep the business relationships between partners . . . well, professional. When the checks and balances of outside help are missing, entrepreneurs often find themselves dealing with issues well outside their skill sets. Balls get dropped. Fingers are pointed. Relationships fray.

The kids don't want to work in the business. "All happy families are alike; each unhappy family is unhappy in its own way." Leo Tolstoy, *Anna Karenina.*

It's not at all uncommon for dad to build a successful business intending to pass it on to his children. It's just as common for the kids to have their own dreams that have nothing to do with dad's business. Between the familial dysfunction, sibling rivalry, and unrealistic parental expectations of vicarious immortality, family business breakups can be among the most complicated and contentious of business disputes.

One partner has baggage. Difficult personal circumstances can have a hugely detrimental impact on your business. Perhaps your partner is going through a messy divorce or has a sick child. Maybe she has a substance abuse problem or serious financial issues. Being helpful and supportive to a business partner during a time of need is noble. But, be cautious about enabling behavior that may harm you or your business. If your business partner has more issues than *National Geographic,* it may be time to cancel your subscription.

IF YOUR BUSINESS PARTNERSHIP ISN'T WORKING, YOU HAVE OPTIONS

Whatever the reason, when a business partnership sours, everything suffers. Running the business becomes more difficult. Profits decline. Your stress level goes up. The quality of your life goes down. Recognizing the problem is the first step to solving it. Once acknowledged, there are three broad ways of addressing the problem of an unproductive business partnership.

Endure it. Some entrepreneurs decide to endure the dysfunction of their business relationship, either because they fear change, or because of inertia. Perhaps the partnership is just functional enough, or just profitable enough, to be worth suffering through. That is certainly a valid choice, particularly if a natural end to the partnership is on the horizon. For example, one partner plans to retire soon, or the business is likely to be acquired in the near term. But, absent the natural horizon, why toil in misery?

Undoubtedly, you've had a crummy job before, in which you were forced to work with people who you didn't like and who made your work harder. In all likelihood, one of the reasons you went into business for yourself was to create your ideal work environment and to control your own destiny. Why let a recalcitrant business partner take that away from you?

Fix it. Sometimes, through candid conversations, a new and more formal delineation of roles and responsibilities, and a renewed commitment to the business, a dysfunctional business partnership can be saved. Just be realistic about the odds of success. Running a business at a profit is hard enough. Trying to do so while also restructuring the business relationship between its owners brings another level of complexity entirely. Imagine trying to renovate a house and reconcile a marriage at the same time. If that sounds feasible, perhaps you are up for salvaging your partnership.

There are a number of consultants who work with closely held companies plagued by dysfunctional relationships in an effort to right the ship while it is still above water. These corporate interventions are perhaps most common when the relationships at issue are both familial and professional.

Even if you are intent on improving, rather than ending, your existing business partnership, you would do well to have an exit strategy. An "out" gives you options, and options are liberating. Having an exit strategy also enables you to negotiate with your partner from a position of strength. Although you may be willing to entertain a restructuring of your business relationship, it is important that your partner understand that you are prepared to walk away. Think of it as ending your existing partnership, and then forming a new partnership with the same partner. But, this time around, you can incorporate what you've learned, keep what worked, and jettison what didn't.

Remember Bonnie and Clyde? I refer to the owners of the tow truck business discussed earlier, not the fugitives from justice. I represented the Clyde in that story. His dispute with Bonnie was headed to a nasty business divorce that would destroy the lucrative business they'd built together. But, cooler heads prevailed. Clyde took my advice, and Bonnie listened to her lawyer, too. We sat down and renegotiated their business relationship from scratch, and we put it in writing. With a new agreement in place, Bonnie and Clyde committed to meeting over breakfast every Friday morning and going through a specific agenda so that each knew what the other had done over the past week, and what each planned to do in the coming week. This one step, more than any other, saved their business.

End it. By the time business partners realize (or are willing to admit) that they have a problem between them, the relationship is often beyond repair. Ending a business partnership while keeping the business, your assets, and your sanity intact can be daunting, but it is also not uncharted territory. Others have done it successfully, and so can you. Life's too short for a bad business partner. This book will help you through it.

TAKE STOCK

Like any other journey, it is important when leaving a business relationship to know both where you are and where you want to go.

Where are you now? Before undertaking the upheaval associated with a business breakup, take stock of where you are today. Are you facing other challenges beyond a dysfunctional business partnership? Aging parents? A rocky marriage? If your challenges are several and severe and if your business partnership is serviceable if not flawless, you may do well to postpone a confrontation with your partner until you get the other aspects of your life under control. It is possible to fight a war on two fronts, but it's not ideal. Do you have a financial cushion, or are you robbing Peter to pay Paul? Take stock and give yourself an unvarnished, but non-judgmental assessment of your current situation so that you can prepare accordingly.

Where do you want to go? "If you don't know where you're going, you'll end up someplace else." Yogi Berra.

In all likelihood, your partner has done something, or has failed to do something, to invoke your ire. Maybe he doesn't pull his weight. Maybe she regularly charges personal expenses on the company's credit card. Perhaps two partners are ganging up to freeze you out. These issues are important, but they are also about the past. These circumstances explain how you got here, but have little to do with where you want to go. The past should not be your focus. The future should be. Do you want to stay in this business for another ten years, serving the same customers out of the same location? Or are you on the verge of retirement, looking to cash out?

Whatever the reason, your business relationship is ending. If you could fix it, you would have. Understanding what went wrong with the partnership is valuable, but dwelling on it is unproductive. Focus on the future.

CHAPTER 2

Amass Your Forces: Information is Power

At some point, you will need to have a conversation, and perhaps a confrontation, with your partner about restructuring or ending your partnership. Before you do so, you would do well to understand the nuts and bolts of that business relationship. Knowledge is power. Understanding what rights, obligations, challenges, and opportunities are in play will enable you to avoid pitfalls along the way. The first step is gathering information.

BUILD A DATABASE

To navigate your way out of a maze, a map is invaluable. Contracts, correspondence, and business financials are the DNA of your business partnership. Gather whatever documents relate to your rights in, and obligations to, the business. Put these materials in one place; a three-ring notebook, in the cloud, whatever works for you. Don't worry too much about analyzing the information at this stage. Just compile it in an organized way that is easily accessible to you.

GATHER KEY DOCUMENTS

You and your business partner have rights against, and obligations to, each other and to the business you own together. You may have similar rights or obligations to landlords, lenders, vendors, and customers. Sometimes these rights are formally memorialized in shareholders agreements, personal guarantees, employment contracts, and other contracts. Maybe it's just in an email or written on the back of a napkin. Whatever the format, gather this information.

Partnership agreements. Among the documents you want to compile are contracts governing the relationships between and among the co-owners of the business. These documents go by different titles depending on the type of entity through which the business operates. Shareholder Agreements govern the relationships between shareholders in a corporation. Operating Agreements govern the relationships between members in a limited liability company. Partnership Agreements memorialize the relationships between partners in a partnership. For simplicity, these agreements between the co-owners of the business will be referred to generically as partnership agreements throughout this book. These partnership agreements are often filled with legalese and references to Byzantine tax codes, but they can be very important in determining the rights and obligations as between the partners and the company.

Employment agreements. If you or your business partner are employed by the company, and you have written employment agreements, those are also documents you want to gather. They may address compensation, rights on termination, or post-employment obligations such as to preserve company secrets, not to compete, or not to solicit customers.

If your business has contracts with non-owner employees, gather those documents as well. The decisions you make about your future may have profound effects on your employees as well. Are those employees likely to stay with you, go with your partner, or leave the business entirely? Is the business viable without them? Are your employees owed deferred compensation? These factors may impact your exit from the business, or that of your partner.

Customer contracts. It is also useful to understand the company's obligations to its clients and customers. Are there long-term contracts with customers that must be fulfilled? If you and your business partner part ways, will the business still be able to service customers, fulfill outstanding orders, and maintain relationships? Do you care? Do you intend to keep the business, or perhaps to service these customers with another business you start or join? These questions are both practical and legal.

Practically, if you want to maintain the relationship, you'll need to factor in how to keep the customer happy while you wind up your business partnership. Legally, if you are bound by a restrictive covenant that would preclude you from soliciting business from the client after you leave, you must either abide by it, negotiate your way out of it, or risk being sued. Similarly, if the business is obligated to provide products or services to a customer and cannot do so as a result of your split with your business partner, the business could become liable to that customer for breach of contract, significantly diminishing its value.

Agreements with vendors, lenders, and landlords. Gather documents that memorialize the company's relationships with its vendors. Does your business get regular product or raw materials deliveries from a supplier? Does the company lease vehicles or equipment? Does it have rent or loan repayment obligations? Did you or your partner personally guaranty those obligations? Obligations like these may impact your freedom of movement. With a solid understanding of your current rights and obligations, you can craft an exit strategy that leverages your opportunities and avoids pitfalls.

Company financials and income tax returns. The whole point of the company is to make you money, so it's a good idea to understand the company's financial situation. To the extent that you have online access to the company's various bank accounts, print out the last few statements for easy reference. Gather up the financial statements for the past few years as well. Do the same with the company's tax returns. A common area of dispute between business owners is who owns how much of the company. The K-1 will reveal, at the very least, the percentage ownership on which the various owners have been reporting to the IRS. Often, the company's accountant can provide this information to you.

Download a comprehensive list of the types of contracts

and other documents you should gather and organize in anticipation of ending or restructuring your business partnership at www.williampiercy.com/resources.

Whenever possible, track down the signed copy of contracts. This will ensure that the document you are reading is actually the one that governs the business relationship. Also important is correspondence between the owners or others that may identify or describe the issues that give rise to the friction within the business.

Create a Narrative Timeline

Write out a chronology identifying the history of your troubled business relationship from its inception. Include key dates and events like formation, capital infusions, contracts signed, store openings, key hires, dates of loans taken and/or retired, key customers won or lost, disputed events, etc. This information will help you organize your thoughts, and may be useful to your attorney and other professionals as they work with you through this process.

Determine Your Role in the Business

Many entrepreneurs are so focused on helping the business grow that they never develop a full understanding of their role in it. Generally, there are four broad categories of involvement in a business enterprise: owner, employee, independent contractor, and creditor. One individual commonly holds more than one of these titles concurrently. In assessing your rights, obligations, challenges, and opportunities in extricating yourself from your existing business relationship, it is important to understand your current role.

Owner. Business owners are generally the individuals or entities who own some or all of the entity through which business is conducted. Owners typically have a say in the management of the business, a right to a share in the profits, and a right to inspect the company's books and records.

The nature of your contractual arrangement and the percentage of the company you own will have a great impact on how much say you have in its operations and management. Some owners are actively involved in the operations of the business. Others are passive investors. Although this is an over simplification, an owner generally only owes fiduciary duties to the company if he has a role in its management. This fiduciary duty may keep an owner from competing with the company, steering opportunities away from it, or acting contrary to its interests.

An owner often receives a K-1 from the company each year for filing with his federal income tax return. That document will identify the percentage of the company owned by the individual and what distributions he may have received over the previous year, among other information. K-1s can be important documents in understanding and asserting your ownership rights. Pay careful attention to the ownership percentage indicated to confirm that it remains steady over multiple years, or investigate why it doesn't. A sudden or unexplained shift in purported ownership percentages is a frequent area of dispute among business partners.

Employee. An employee generally works in the service of another person or company for wages or a salary. The employee-employer relationship is governed by either an express or implied contract, under which the employer generally has the right to control certain details of the workplace. Employees can take many different forms—some are salaried, some work on commission, others are paid hourly, some are full time, others are part time—but, all employees are afforded rights under both state and federal law that employers and owners must provide. These include the rights to be free from discrimination and harassment; a safe workplace; be free from retaliation; and fair wages for work performed, wage and hour requirements, workers compensation, and unemployment insurance, and privacy. Additionally, employees are entitled to earn the minimum wage, and are generally entitled to overtime pay in the event that they work more than a standard workweek of 40 hours per week, unless otherwise excepted from the regulations.

Generally, an employee owes a company a duty of loyalty, which could prevent him from moonlighting with a competitor or sharing the company's secrets. This can vary widely from state to state. Unless a written contract states otherwise, employment relationships are generally "at-will" such that employers and employees may terminate the employment relationship at will for nearly any non-discriminatory reason without penalty.

Employers are required by federal law to withhold employment taxes from an employee's salary and to issue the employee a W-2 each year, identifying the income the employee received from the company in the preceding year.

Independent contractor. An independent contractor is a person or entity who provides labor or other services, but who retains substantial autonomy as to how those services are provided. The nature of the relationship is defined by contract. An independent contractor receives payment for services without the withholding of employment taxes and should receive a 1099 from the company confirming the amounts paid within a given year.

Creditor. If you've loaned money to your company, separate and apart from any money you've paid to the company in exchange for an ownership interest, you are likely a creditor. Sometimes these transactions are memorialized formally in a promissory note or other loan document. Other times, an entrepreneur covers a company expense with personal funds, and then seeks reimbursement when the company is able to afford it. A creditor is entitled to repayment for the principal loaned, plus interest.

Blurred lines. What happens when a person holds multiple titles? Despite the sometimes fuzzy line between these roles, the law continues to recognize distinctions between them. In other words, if one person is an owner, an employee, and a creditor, he is generally afforded the rights and obligations of each.

SOLIDIFY RELATIONSHIPS WITH GATEKEEPERS

Once you've gathered the contracts and other documents that relate to the business, make a list of the people who are important to this business. Inside the business, this list will typically include the other owners, as well as the employees. External to the business, this list may include a CPA, the relationship manager or loan officer at the company's bank, the landlord, the company's information technology provider, and the day-to-day contact person at the company's best customers and vendors. For a list of the types of folks with whom you may want to build or solidify a rapport before approaching your business partner about separating, download it at www.williampiercy.com/resources.

You may know some of these people well. If you handled the company's IT needs, chances are, you know the tech rep and he knows you. But, if your partner historically pays the rent and makes calls asking for roof repairs or rent concessions, you might have no idea who the property manager is or how to reach him. You would do well to find out who these people are and how to get in touch with them before issues with your partner deteriorate any further.

An unfortunate, but common action arising from a failing business partnership is that one or more partners will take steps to lock or freeze another partner out. They change the password for the online bank account, or company server, or the lock on the front door. If you've never communicated with the company's banker, it's going to take a lot more effort to talk her into giving you access to the company's online accounts over your partner's objections than if she's met you several times before. The same is true with the IT vendor tech rep, the landlord, and others vital to the operations of your business. If possible, take the time to get to know these people before your partnership deteriorates to the point that the only communications between partners are peppered with four-letter words.

A word of caution about talking to other people about the business partner with whom you no longer share a common vision, and whom you perhaps can no longer stand. There's a good chance that, at some point in your childhood, your mother told you that if you can't say something nice about someone, don't say anything at all. That advice holds true when talking about the business partner who has become a thorn in your side. There are three reasons for this. First, your mother said so. Second, you want to preserve the value of your business. Oversharing about problems in the business or between its owners does nothing to create confidence in your business. Third, you don't want to get sued for defamation.

Similarly, inviting current customers of your company to begin doing business with a new company you intend to start is a sure way to get sued for usurpation of corporate opportunity or breach of fiduciary duty.

INVENTORY COMPANY ASSETS AND LIABILITIES

When a marriage ends in divorce, spouses inevitably create a list of the stuff to be divided between them. Do the same with the assets and liabilities of your business. This will give you some sense of what is to be divvied up, sold, purchased, or otherwise accounted for when going through a business divorce.

In compiling the list, consider cash, real estate, long-term contracts, and intellectual property. Intellectual property may include patents, copyright or trademark registrations, business plans, customer lists, pricing lists, and other business intelligence. Do not underestimate the importance of this step. You can find a list of assets and liabilities you may want to identify by visiting www.williampiercy.com/resources.

A word now about the distinction between owning a portion of a business and owning the assets of that business. Owning some portion of a business does not give you an ownership interest in the assets of the business. This is true not only of your company's money and physical assets, but of its intellectual property as well.

All too often, a business owner, frustrated with a partner's greed or incompetence, emails the company's customer and pricing lists to his personal email account, either for "safe keeping" or to start a new competing business. This is a sure way to get sued for misappropriation of trade secrets, conversion, misappropriation of corporate assets, or usurpation of corporate opportunity. Do not help yourself to company property or data. Particularly when your partner is being difficult, it can be tempting to help yourself to an extra distribution, or to forward the company's customer list to your personal email account. Resist the urge. You might own a piece of the company, but company property belongs to the company. Taking it will get you sued.

Sorting out whether property is personal or corporate is no easy task, and given the risks of taking property that does not belong to you, it's worth working with a lawyer to help you sort it out. Some factors to consider in making the determination of ownership are: How is the asset titled? Who paid for it? Is the asset declared on a personal or corporate balance sheet or financial statement? Has it been depreciated or deducted off of a personal or corporate tax return? Armed with this information, you can move forward to the next phase of ending your bad business relationship.

Final Thoughts on Amassing Data and Befriending Gatekeepers

Once you have gathered the materials and solidified the relationships discussed in this chapter, read through them and get a general sense of what you've compiled. If there are gaps, do what you can to track down missing materials. But, recognize that you'll never have all the information you want when it comes to making difficult decisions. A corporate divorce is no place for a perfectionist. Get comfortable with 80 percent solutions.

CHAPTER 3

Assemble a Team, Analyze the Data, and Prepare for What's Next

Once you've determined that the status quo is unacceptable and gathered all possible information relevant to your business, the next step is to analyze that information so that you can use it to your advantage. The emphasis is on *preparing* rather than on *planning*. As battle hardened veterans will tell you, no plan survives first contact with the enemy. Plans go off the rails. But, robust preparation makes you ready for whatever comes next.

ASSEMBLE A TEAM

Although this book will help you navigate a business breakup, it is by no means the only support you should seek. Assemble a team of professionals and trusted advisors to assist you. Depending on your network and your needs, you'll need to pay some of these folks. Look for people who will be supportive without being enablers. You don't need yes-men who reaffirm your conviction that your partner is a jerk. You need someone who will listen, offer constructive feedback, and perhaps provide you with some tough love.

Business lawyer. A good lawyer is an essential part of your team. A lawyer will help you understand the contracts you've signed, and alert you to the laws and doctrines applicable to your situation.

Particularly if you have never done so before, hiring a lawyer can be daunting. Take your time. Interview at least two. Ask questions. Pay attention to the answers.

Nothing is more expensive than a cheap lawyer. Expect to pay an hourly rate, and a retainer up front. Business disputes are generally not good candidates for contingency fee arrangements because unlike a personal injury case, there is rarely a large insurance company involved that must write a check to the winner. The hourly rate a lawyer charges is often reflective of the attorney's experience. It may well be that a lawyer who charges $400 per hour can complete a task in half the time (and perhaps twice as well) as one who does so for less. Like most things in life, when it comes to hiring a lawyer, you generally get what you pay for.

Accountant. An accountant can help you understand the financial statements of your business and create them if they don't exist. That accountant can also spot trends or irregularities in your company's financials that you may have missed. This could help uncover problems in your business, or perhaps improprieties perpetrated by your partner or employees.

Industry professional. Particularly if you intend to stay in the business, or in the same industry, you would do well to talk to someone with broad industry experience about what's next for you. This might be a good time to revamp your business model, streamline your service offering, and reassess who may be your best clients. It is easy to put blinders on and to assume the way you've been doing business is the way it should continue to be done. Clearly, your partner is not going to help you see what's on the horizon. Find someone who can.

Mentor. Like the industry professional, a mentor can bring long-term perspective, which can be a healthy thing during the short-term crisis. As a trusted advisor, your mentor should pose questions for you to consider, share insights you might not have thought of, make recommendations, or introduce you to key individuals who can help. A good mentor may also help you understand your role in a dysfunctional partnership. That sort of advice isn't always easy to hear, but it will certainly reduce the risk of repeating past mistakes.

Banker. Things might happen fast during the transition of your business relationship. You would do well to have a friendly banker who can help you understand and access credit options and other banking needs. It may be wise to work with someone at a different bank from the one your business currently uses. She may help you understand options and even compete for your business in a way that an entrenched banker will not. Indeed, the banker with whom you already have a relationship may be terrified at the prospect of a business breakup, particularly if the bank has extended credit to your business. You don't need any more adversaries.

A friend who will listen. Sometimes you just need someone who will lend an ear or a shoulder and who will listen without judgment. Barring that, get a dog.

Business broker. If selling your business to an outsider is an option, enlist the help of a professional who regularly brings businesses to market. For selling your business to even be a possibility, it must be worth something to an outsider. A business broker can help the business look its best to a prospective purchaser. If you hope to sell your business, you will likely also need the consent and cooperation of your partner. A business broker who can work with finicky buyers, while simultaneously working with a group of sellers who are in a dispute with one another, earns every penny of his fee.

Valuation specialist. For what it is worth, you may want a professional to determine the value of your business. An accurate valuation of your business can help you decide whether it's worth fighting for, and that's no small thing. A valuation can also bring credibility and reason to your discussions with a partner about how much one should pay the other for his share of the business in a buyout scenario.

ANALYZE THE DATA

With the appropriate team member, read through and digest the documents you've gathered. Ask your accountant if he sees anything amiss in the bank statements or the general ledger. Review the contracts with your lawyer and ask questions. Then, read them again and ask more questions.

Entrepreneurs commonly complain that the contract the partners signed does not match the reality on the ground. Notwithstanding that perspective, the contract says what it says and will generally be enforced as written. Given that, a working understanding of some of the more common provisions that appear in contracts affecting your rights with respect to the business and your business partners is helpful. Below are brief descriptions of several provisions that can have an outsized impact on your rights, obligations, and bargaining power.

Ownership percentages. Generally, a partnership agreement will specify who owns how much of the company. This information can often be found in an appendix. This percentage often correlates with the weight of your vote on company matters and also the percentage of profits you are entitled to receive come distribution time.

Where the contract does not specify who owns how much of the company (or there is no written contract), the information can often be gleaned from tax records such as K-1s, or perhaps on the company's capital account records.

Voting rights. The partnership agreement may specify whether each owner gets an equal vote, or if their votes are proportional to their ownership interests. Many corporations have non-voting shares, and LLCs may have economic interests that entitle the owner to a proportional share of profits, but provide for no say in the operation of the business. Some agreements call for actions to be taken upon the vote of a super majority (i.e. some percentage greater than 50 percent). Determining who owns how much, and how much of a voting block is required to take certain actions, can be determinative of who has the right to act on behalf of the company.

Management. Who is in charge of the day-to-day operations of the business? Some agreements identify a specific person. Others identify how and when those persons are appointed or removed from office. Corporations are typically managed by a president and/or a chief executive officer. LLCs are typically managed either by a manager or by a majority vote of the members, and partnerships by a majority vote of partners or by a designated managing partner.

Contractual provisions related to management may also impose limitations on a manager's authority to perform certain tasks. These limitations might also impact one's authority to spend or borrow up to a limit, beyond which, a vote or unanimous consent of all owners is required. Understanding these rights and limits can provide significant leverage in the termination negotiations.

Owners with management authority may find that role to be both a blessing and a curse. With that authority comes control over the operations and resources of the business. But, that authority is also tempered by a fiduciary duty to exercise that control in the best interests of the business and its other owners, regardless how one may feel about them.

Distribution of profits and other compensation. Often, a partnership agreement will specify when, or conditions under which, profits of the company must or may be distributed to owners. Some distributions are guaranteed, others are based on formulas related to the ratio of income and expenses. A provision may require distributions to cover tax obligations imposed on the company's owners by virtue of their ownership. Other distributions are left entirely to the discretion of management. There may also be specific reference to compensation paid to an owner in exchange for fulfilling a role within the company. For example, if an owner is also the president, she may be entitled to both a salary for managing the company, as well as profit distributions resulting from her ownership interest. Understanding the criteria around distributions can help establish what money and assets you may be entitled to, or help you determine whether money your partner has taken out of the business was improper.

Buyout. Partnership agreements often contain provisions allowing for the company, or a partner, to purchase the ownership interests of another partner in the business. The buyout is often linked to a separate provision that governs how the value of an interest is to be determined. Buyout provisions can be hugely important in the partnership's dissolution process and are often a source of tension and disputes.

Buy-sell. A common provision found in agreements between two owner companies is a buy-sell provision, sometimes referred to as a "shotgun provision" or the "Sword of Damocles." With the 'shotgun' or 'sword' provision, one owner can make an offer to purchase the ownership interest of the other at whatever price he chooses. The recipient of that offer then has a fixed time in which to accept the proposal as offered, or to reverse it, such that the recipient becomes the buyer and the owner initiating the offer becomes the seller, on the same terms as the original offer. The provision is designed to ensure that proposals are fair, in that the initiating owner does not know whether he'll be buying or selling when he sets the price. But, it can also lead to a high stakes game of "chicken".

The attempt to exercise rights under these shotgun provisions frequently leads to litigation about the enforceability of the provision, the good faith of the proposal, or a myriad other issues. While these provisions are meant to be an efficient way of reaching a fair buyout number, there are ways to game the system, and nobody likes to play games more than an entrepreneur who no longer cares what his partner thinks of him. For example, if one partner has considerably more money than the other, he may make a low-ball offer to his partner, believing that even at that unfair price, his partner can't afford to buy him out.

Alternatively, it may make far more sense for one partner to continue with the business, or perhaps one partner is just more attached to it. The other partner could take advantage of this fact, offering to buy the business for an exorbitant sum with the hope that his partner will feel compelled to flip the offer and buy him out at that price. The risks of these strategies should be obvious, but people take them all the time.

For example, Bo and Luke were equal partners in a promotional products company (PPC). The PPC operating agreement contained a shotgun provision like that described above.

Bo, tired of Luke's reckless spending and inattention to cash flow, tried to have a productive conversation with Luke about separating their business interests. But Luke blew him off. Bo exercised his right under the shotgun provision. Bo didn't know whether Luke would buy or sell, so he hedged his bets and made a middle of the road offer. Luke elected to sell out. But, before closing, Luke surreptitiously emailed the PPC's customer and pricing lists to his personal email account. This information was a significant PPC asset, developed over many years at great expense. By taking this information just before being bought out, Luke effectively sucked much of the value out of the company. Luke had his cake and ate it too.

Within a month of the closing, Luke opened a competing business. But, Luke made a mistake. When he emailed a solicitation for his new business to the clients and prospects of the PPC, he inadvertently also sent that email to Bo's personal email address. Because Bo typically handled the PPC's marketing initiatives, he (Bo) included his personal email address in the company's database so that when a mass email went out, he would receive it as a quality control measure. In this instance, it was the canary in the coal mine.

Bo hired me to recover the value he'd lost as a result of Luke's subterfuge. We hired a computer forensics expert, who promptly discovered Luke's misappropriation of the PPC customer and pricing lists. Armed with this information, Bo sued Luke, and eventually negotiated a favorable settlement. Although Bo was eventually made whole, this story highlights one example of how an unscrupulous business partner can take advantage of his partner on the way out the door.

Valuation. Many partnership agreements allow the company or one of its owners to purchase the ownership interest of another at a price based on a contractual formula, or at a price set by an appraiser appointed by some mechanism of varying complexity. Sometimes, the contract provides that the valuation is automatically diminished (often halved) for buyout purposes if the exiting partner undertook some malfeasance detrimental to the company, or is accused of criminal activity. Understanding the workings of a valuation clause is critical in assessing your bargaining power.

Involuntary transfers. Many partnership agreements either allow or require the company to acquire one owner's interest in the business if he or she becomes disabled, gets divorced, files for bankruptcy, is convicted of a crime, or engages in behavior detrimental to the business.

This final, and very subjective trigger, often leads to highly contested and contentious ownership terminations. If an owner unwittingly triggers an involuntary transfer obligation, it can create substantial leverage for the other owners in the business should they be looking for a reason to get rid of the triggering partner.

Restrictive covenants. Many partnership agreements restrict an owner's ability to engage in activities commercially competitive with the business, either while they are a member, or for some period after they divest their ownership interest. Others expressly allow an owner or former owner to engage in competitive activities. The enforceability of these provisions varies widely from state to state. Typically, the less restrictive the provision, the more likely it is enforceable. These restrictive covenant provisions come in four main varieties.

> **Confidentiality:** This provision requires the members to maintain the confidentiality of the business's proprietary information and not to use the company's information or resources for any purpose other than the advancement of the business's best interests.
>
> **Non-Compete:** These provisions typically preclude an owner from engaging in a particular activity related to the business of the company within a specific region for a set period.
>
> **Non-Solicitation:** A non-solicitation provision typically precludes an owner from soliciting business from certain people who did business with the company (typically the current clients of the business of which he is an owner) for a specific period.

Non-Recruitment: Similar to a non-solicit, a non-recruitment provision precludes an owner from attempting to hire away employees from the business for a competing venture, or perhaps from doing business with certain vendors, during his ownership and for some time after his divesture of that ownership.

If your goal is to leave your business, but to continue to work in the same industry and in the same area, a restrictive covenant is a hurdle to overcome. You'll either need to negotiate your way out of it, sit in the penalty box until the covenant expires, or challenge the covenant in court and win the right to compete. The inverse is true if it is your former business partner who is restricted by the covenant. Either way, one of you will have significant negotiating leverage. You want to know this before you begin your negotiation.

Dispute resolution. Absent a provision to the contrary, an owner's method of seeking compensation for a wrong inflicted upon him by his co-owner, or the business of which he owns a part, is to file a lawsuit. Many agreements between business owners elect one or more alternative dispute resolution methods. These provisions take many forms, but often address some or all of the following topics.

Mediation: Mediation is a process whereby a mediator (often an old warhorse lawyer or a retired judge) facilitates a negotiation between the disputing parties in an effort to reach a resolution. Think Kissinger at Camp David. If the parties reach a deal, an agreement is drafted and signed and it is binding on the parties. If the parties are unable to agree, they are free to sue each other in court or in arbitration, as the case may be. Mediation is hugely effective in bringing business disputes to creative resolution. It allows the parties to control the outcome, rather than having one foisted upon them by a judge or jury who will never know as much about their business, or their circumstances, as the parties to the dispute. It also allows the parties to craft business minded solutions that are outside the power of a judge or jury to award. Often, the biggest roadblock to a successful mediation is getting both parties to participate meaningfully. With the right leverage, this is an obstacle that can often be overcome.

Arbitration: Arbitration is a binding dispute resolution process in which a third party neutral, an arbitrator (or a panel of them), hears evidence and then makes a decision that is binding on the parties. It's similar to court except that instead of a judge (paid by taxpayers) making the decisions, the arbitrator (paid by the parties in the dispute) is the "decider". There are legions of articles on the pros and cons of arbitration and I will not reiterate the relative merits here. Suffice it to say that arbitration is advantageous for some disputes and not for others. If your agreement requires dispute resolution by binding arbitration, you may be stuck arbitrating whether you want to be there or not.

Forum selection. The default rule (to which there are, of course, exceptions) in litigation is that a defendant has the right to be sued in the jurisdiction in which he resides. However, it is possible to waive this right by contract. If you and your partners live locally, this is likely not an issue. But, where co-owners are far flung, a forum selection provision can be very important. If you reside in Georgia, your partner is in Illinois, and your agreement contains an Illinois forum selection provision, you could find yourself litigating in your erstwhile partner's backyard, much to your inconvenience.

Attorney's fees. To the surprise of many, the default rule is that everyone pays their own attorney's fees in the resolution of business disputes in court. Business owners can and often do replace this default rule with a contractual term allowing a judge, jury, or arbitrator to award fees to the prevailing party in any dispute between them. In other words, loser pays. The potential shift of this expense can be an important factor to consider when negotiating the end of a partnership.

Entire agreement clause. Most contracts between and among business partners contain an entire agreement provision. Basically, this clause states that regardless what the parties may have agreed to, promised, or represented to each other in the past, everyone agrees that the only agreements, promises, and representations that remain binding are those contained in the agreement in which this clause is present. This circumvents many claims based on old history and helps parties "clean up" negotiations so that everyone is clear as to what is being agreed to and relied upon. It is all but impossible to assert a claim for fraud based on promises that pre-date, and that are not contained in, a contract containing an entire agreement clause.

Any of these provisions can have a profound effect on your negotiating leverage. For that reason, you want to understand how these and other provisions in your agreement affect your situation. A good lawyer can help you understand these impacts and the opportunities and challenges they present.

MAKE A WIND-UP TO-DO LIST

Whether you are leaving the business, keeping it, selling it, or closing it down, there are a myriad of loose ends you need to tie up to ensure that your past doesn't interfere with your future. Are there loans, leases, or other long-term obligations to be factored into an exit plan? Perhaps there are insurance policies to cancel, or transfer. Are there customers or employees you don't want to leave in a lurch? Maybe there are just piles of money to distribute. Whatever your circumstances, make a list so as to ensure that all the loose ends get tied off. The goal is to identify and eventually to deal with every obstacle between you and a clean exit from your current business relationships. You can download a template list of wind-up issues to address at www.williampiercy.com/resources.

PREPARE FOR CHANGE

The next chapter of this book provides guidance on negotiating effectively with your business partner. Before you enter into that negotiation, you should put yourself in a position to succeed by preparing for inevitable change. To the extent possible, free yourself of other distractions. Trim your expenses. Set aside a little cash. Get ready for the whirlwind.

Think through where you want to be, not in a week, but in a year. Consider two or three alternative paths to that destination. For example, you may want to stay in the same industry in the same part of town. One option for getting there might be to buy out your business partner and to keep running the same business. Another option might be to agree to be bought out and not to solicit the company's clients or to otherwise compete with it for a year. During that year, you might travel, go back to school, or lean a new skill. When the year is up, you'll be rested, refreshed, and able to resume your place at the top of your chosen industry. In both circumstances, you end up in the same place after a year, despite taking two entirely different routes to get there.

If you suspect that your partner may react poorly to the news that you want out, prepare for that eventuality before breaking the news. Certainly, this entails compiling the information described in this chapter. You might also want to remove your personal effects from the office and set yourself up to work remotely for a time. This is not to say you should not go to the office. It is perhaps more important than ever that you keep your finger on the pulse of your business. But, if you can accomplish this by stopping in a few days a week and keeping in regular contact with employees, you can avoid the tension and stress of spending long hours in the office with a partner you find it difficult to look at without the balling of fists and the gnashing of teeth.

Based on the information you've gathered, the contracts you've analyzed, and the other relationships you have in place, make a list of your challenges and opportunities. Perhaps your partner has more money with which to wage a court battle, but you are confident that the company's clients will follow you wherever you go. Maybe you've got great credit and your partner recently filed bankruptcy. Perhaps your industry is changing and margins are shrinking. Be honest with, but not hard on, yourself in creating this list. It will help you craft an exit negotiation strategy.

Change is the only constant. Prepare for it.

CHAPTER 4

Negotiate from a Position of Strength

You've accepted that you need a change. You've gathered your documents, solidified your relationships, consulted with your team, and prepared yourself for the coming storm. Now is the time for deliberate action.

THE CONVERSATION: TELL YOUR BUSINESS PARTNER YOU WANT OUT

In all but the most egregious and dysfunctional of circumstances, you should communicate with your business partner, and tell him that you want out. Depending on your situation, this may be the easiest or the hardest part of this process.

If you can stomach it, do it in person, briefly, suggesting a later time to meet again to work through the logistics. If that will not work for you, send a short email explaining your desire to separate, and suggest a follow-up meeting or dialogue. Practice with a friend, or give them a draft of your correspondence and a red pen so they can delete all of the passive-aggressive parts that you are too angry to see. As tempting as it may be, this conversation is not the time to air your grievances. Doing so will only make your partner defensive and invite invective back on you.

Whether you schedule a meeting over coffee or send an email, explain in clear, respectful, non-accusatory terms that the business relationship is no longer working for you. Offer to cooperate in a smooth transition. Give him time to respond before you launch into how you think the transition should occur. You might be surprised at what he has to say. Listen, then politely make your exit. Even if your partner gets nasty, bite your tongue, thank him for his time, tell him you'll be in touch, and leave. Then smile to yourself, knowing that you are in control of your emotions, and your partner is not. You shouldn't go to the grocery store when you're hungry, and you shouldn't negotiate when you're angry. Neither should your partner.

If the initial conversation goes well, schedule a more comprehensive meeting with your partner to talk logistics. Develop a list of talking points. It may look a lot like the wind-up to-do list discussed in Chapter 3 and provided in the downloadable resource. If face-to-face dialogue will be uncomfortable to the point of being disruptive, continue your dialogue via email or through counsel. Again, have your lawyer, or a friend, review what you plan to send to keep it sanitized. Don't be the one who lights the dumpster fire. And if your partner lights one, don't add fuel to it. Spilling raw emotions in an angry outburst or email might feel good at the moment, but that outburst might cost you tens of thousands of dollars in legal fees, not to mention opportunities and even lost sanity. Keep it civil. You'll be glad you did.

THE NEGOTIATION: START FROM A POSITION OF STRENGTH

Chances are, someone older and wiser than you—a teacher, a coach, your mother—said these words to you when you felt compelled to do something you didn't want to do: "You always have a choice." You can choose to get up in the morning or stay in bed all day. Your choice may be to move to another state, or to work in another industry, or to stay in the same rut you've been stuck in for the past six months. The choice is yours. That said, choice isn't free. There is a cost associated with every choice you make. Being prepared to pay the price of that choice is the key to negotiating from a position of strength.

What does this mean? It means being willing to accept the consequences of a hard choice. Perhaps your first option would be to buy out your business partner at a fair price and to keep running the business yourself. Like it or not, your business partner probably knows this would be your first choice. With that knowledge, he may also feel empowered to demand a premium for his interest in the business because he knows how much you want it. You can get mad about this if you want, but it won't change anything. Allow yourself to be mad. Break something. Then take a deep breath and accept this reality.

Next, prepare yourself to do something other than your first choice. This does not mean settling for less; it means being flexible about getting where you want to go. By demonstrating a willingness to pursue a path different than your first choice, you show your business partner that you have options, and that you are willing to exercise them. This significantly strengthens your bargaining power and diminishes his.

In the same way that you can't fake authenticity, faking resolve won't work either. Many a business owner will bluff by threatening a scorched earth litigation in an effort to scare their partner into unconditional surrender, even though they lack the time, stomach, or money to follow through on that threat. Your partner is not as dumb as you think he is. In fact, he might even be as smart as you thought he was when you first formed a partnership with him. Nothing will destroy your credibility faster than making empty threats on which you are unwilling to follow through. If you are going to offer a concession or to make a threat, be prepared to deliver. Getting yourself in this frame of mind—one that is both flexible and willing to accept the consequences of hard choices—will do wonders for your bargaining power. It's not easy, but it's simple.

CARROTS AND STICKS: THE YIN AND YANG OF EFFECTIVE NEGOTIATION

Negotiating the end of a business partnership is fundamentally different than the negotiations that lead to a partnership's creation. The fact that you are trying to negotiate your way out of a partnership is an indication that you and your partner either don't want the same things or cannot agree on how to get there. In business breakups, effective negotiations often require that you incentivize your former partner to cooperate in the dissolution of your partnership.

A "carrots and sticks" approach can be effective when employed properly. "Carrots" are the things you are willing to offer that your partner wants. "Sticks" are the threats of negative consequences you are willing to impose on your partner if you and he do not come to an agreement through negotiation.

Using one or the other is unlikely to get you very far. It is the combination of the two that is effective. If you keep offering carrots, your partner, like a rabbit, will just eat until he is full and then hop off without offering you anything in return. Alternatively, if your strategy is focused solely on swinging sticks, your partner will likely conclude that he has little to gain and everything to lose by not fighting back. Instead of cowering in a corner, your former partner, and current adversary, is likely to pick up a stick and swing it back at you. Even if you can take him, is that really how you want to spend your time? You went into business to gain some control over your life, to earn a living, to provide for your family, and to take great vacations. You didn't start this business so you could fight it out with your partner.

Carrots: The Tastier the Better

The information gathering and soul-searching exercises described above will help you figure out the result you want and determine the leverage you have to achieve it. Although it may seem counterintuitive, consider what your business partner would want if she performed the same analysis. This is not altruism; it is sound negotiation strategy. The more you understand your partner's goals, interests, limitations, and opportunities, the more negotiating power you have. Good negotiation is looking out for your own interests while framing your communications in terms of the interests of the person with whom you are negotiating. What can you offer your erstwhile partner that he both wants and that you have the power to give? That's your carrot. Common negotiation carrots include:

Cold, hard cash. What price would you be willing to pay for your partner's ownership interest in the business? Alternatively, at what price would you be willing to sell yours? Would you accept or make payments over time? If so, what security could you offer, or would you insist upon to ensure that those payments are made?

Restrictive covenants. Perhaps you could agree to release a partner from certain restrictive covenants, or to limit their scope. You could agree to allow your partner the right to take a list of customer relationships with him when he leaves. Alternatively, you could agree to be bound by a restrictive covenant for some period of time (i.e. that you would not take or pursue a customer or prospect for a period, or that you would not compete in a particular region or industry for a time). With a little creative flexibility, restrictive covenants can be a powerful negotiating tool when it comes to exiting a business relationship.

Dividing assets. Maybe the business owns a truck, or a printing press, or a database that you can afford to be without, but that your partner very much wants. Allowing him to take those assets as part of his departure, or to keep them upon yours, may be a tasty carrot you can offer up.

Release of claims. If your partner has acted in such a way as to give rise to legal claims against him, your agreement not to pursue those claims can be a powerful incentive for him to do or give you something that you want.

Carry a Big Stick

When negotiating with foreign powers, U.S. President Theodore Roosevelt described his strategy as "Speak softly and carry a big stick." Sticks are the negative consequences you are willing to impose on your erstwhile partner if you are not able to reach an amicable resolution of your disputes. They are a vital part of the negotiating process. Sticks represent what your partner stands to lose by not working things out with you. Some negotiating sticks include:

Insist on reviewing business records. Chapter 6 discusses your right to inspect the books and records of your business. Particularly if it has been a long time since you have had access to the company's bank and credit card statements, demanding to see them—and implicitly threatening to shine the light of day on your partner's activities—may be a very powerful threat.

Force a buyout. If your partnership agreement contains a mandatory buyout provision, you may be able to invoke your right to sell your interest or alternatively to buy your partner out. These contractual provisions were discussed in Chapter 3.

Force a dissolution. Whether by contract or statute, you may have the right to force the dissolution of your company. In a judicial dissolution, the assets of the company are gathered and sold at auction. The proceeds are used first to pay the debts of the company, and then divided between its owners, pro rata. This is not an ideal way to sell a business. It is costly, and unlikely to bring a good price. But, it has the distinct advantage of not requiring your partner's consent. In some ways, a judicial dissolution is the nuclear option of mutually assured destruction. If you are prepared to accept the pain of a dissolution more than your partner is, he may just flinch and become more reasonable at the negotiating table. Judicial dissolutions are discussed further in Chapter 5.

Call a loan. If you capitalized the business with a loan from your personal funds, you may have the right to call that loan, forcing the company to repay you, and depriving it of the ability to stay in business. Suddenly, your partner's income stream is threatened and he is forced to be more reasonable in his negotiations with you.

Stop working. If you provide a service or fulfill a role necessary to the day-to-day operations of the business, you generally have the right not to do so. By withholding support for the operations of the business, your partner's income stream may be threatened, but it also means that *your* income stream is threatened. Again, ask yourself if you are prepared to follow through on this threat before making it. You may also be limited in your ability to withhold work by your operating agreement or employment contract. Talk to your lawyer. Figure it out. Make your move.

File a lawsuit. If your partner breached contractual or fiduciary duties to you or to the company, you can bring suit on your own behalf, or on behalf of the company (i.e. derivatively). More on this in Chapter 6. The good and bad news about filing a lawsuit is that a long time generally passes between the time you file suit, and when the case gets to trial. The wait can be painful, and yet, a looming trial date puts pressure on your business partner to negotiate a resolution so as to avoid being taken to court.

Do not threaten a lawsuit if you are not prepared to follow through. This goes back to maintaining credibility as discussed earlier. The goal may be to incentivize your former partner into negotiating or capitulating. But, you must be prepared for the possibility that your partner declines your reasonable overtures to settle. If you lack the time, the money, or the intestinal fortitude to see a lawsuit through to the end, think twice before threatening or filing one. Your bluff might just get called.

Final Thoughts on Negotiation

By approaching your negotiation with an arsenal of carrots and sticks, you greatly increase your chances of incentivizing your partner to come to a reasonable resolution. Understand that negotiations take time. Be patient. There is a reason that car salesmen keep you sitting around the dealership for hours. Doing so increases the chances that they'll make a sale. The same is true in the negotiation of a partnership breakup. Give the process sufficient time to work. Also, consider mediation, a form of dispute resolution discussed in Chapter 3. It works, and may save you time, money, and aggravation in the end.

If possible, resolve your dispute with your partner without resorting to litigation. Give until it hurts. That is not the same thing, however, as giving until you bleed to death. At some point, you've got to dig in your heels. Lean on your team to help you find that line in the sand. If your partner is unwilling to negotiate in good faith, stop trying. Appeasement doesn't work. Part of negotiating from a position of strength is knowing when to stop negotiating. Remember, you have a choice.

CHAPTER 5

Fight to Win

When negotiations fail, and neither staying nor leaving are viable options, it's time to fight. The type of battle I am advocating for here takes place in a courtroom, not a back alley. Through a lawsuit, you may be able to recover damages for malfeasance, resolve disputes about ownership and compensation, and perhaps even dissolve the business and divide its assets. Demonstrating a true resolve to fight can often cause your former partner to blink and to re-open negotiations that you thought were dead and done.

To succeed in litigation, you must have two things: viable legal claims, and the wherewithal to pursue them to trial. To have a valid legal claim against someone, they must have engaged in conduct that caused you or the business harm, or that otherwise justifies judicial intervention.

Legal claims fall into two broad categories: damages claims and equitable claims. Damages claims allow for the recovery of money to compensate for losses. Equitable claims allow a court to require that some action be taken or refrained from being taken. Similarly, courts can make judicial declarations as to the rights and obligations of the litigants going forward. Below are brief descriptions of the most common claims asserted in business disputes.

MONEY DAMAGES CLAIMS

Damages claims are those for which the remedy for the wrongful conduct is money. Following are brief descriptions of the most common damages claims that arise from disputes between business partners.

Breach of contract. A contract is an agreement between two or more parties to do or refrain from doing something in exchange for something else. When one party fails to fulfill his commitment, he has breached the agreement and is liable to the other party to the contract for any monetary damages that result from the breach. You and your business partner have one or more contractual relationships. They may be very formal. Alternatively, your contract may be informal, or even implied. Regardless, if you agreed to a mutual give and take, it's probably a contract.

Breach of fiduciary duty. Officers and directors of a corporation, managers of a limited liability company, and partners in a partnership owe a fiduciary duty to the business and its owners to act in the best interest of the company when they act in their official capacity. Where management takes intentional action that is not in the company's best interest, that duty is breached.

To constitute a breach of fiduciary duty, the conduct must be detrimental to the best interests of the company. Even this is not always enough. The business judgment rule gives broad protection to corporate officers, directors, and managers. The doctrine gives management the presumption that, in making a business decision, managers act in good faith, in an informed manner, and in the best interests of the company and its owners. The rule protects officers from personal liability unless it is proven that a manager acted in bad faith, showed disloyalty to the company, engaged in self-dealing, or otherwise abused his or her discretion in acting on behalf of the business. To rebut the presumption of the rule, an opposing party must show that the decision-making process undertaken by the manager whose conduct is being challenged constitutes gross negligence or a gross deviation from the standard of care of a manager in a similar position under roughly the same circumstances.

Company managers often breach fiduciary duties by engaging in conflicting interest transactions. A conflicting interest transaction benefits the perpetrator specifically, rather than benefitting all owners of the business. An example would be an LLC manager who hires his wife to do the bookkeeping for the company. Such an arrangement is not prohibited, but the law will examine it more closely. If the manager pays his wife a market rate to perform the bookkeeping, the law will not punish the manager. But, if the going rate is $500 per week for such services and the manager is paying his wife $1,500 per week, the manager is likely to be found to have breached his fiduciary duties to the company.

Fraud. Fraud is an intentional deception of another for personal or financial gain at the expense of the defrauded party. Because of the intent element, fraud can be hard to prove. Many potential fraud claims are precluded by an entire agreement clause in the contracts between the parties. That said, if a viable fraud claim does exist, it can be a powerful one, often allowing not only for the recovery of compensatory damages, but punitive damages and attorney's fees as well.

Conversion. Conversion is the civil remedy for theft. If your partner stole from you or the business, conversion is your remedy. For the moment, put the thought of calling the police or pressing criminal charges on hold. That issue is addressed in Chapter 6. One challenge with bringing a conversion claim is proving ownership of the converted property. Is it yours? Your partner's? Does it belong to the company? Another issue in bringing a conversion claim is identifying a specific item of property that was converted. This is easy if the property is a company truck. But, when the property is data, or even money, the challenge is much greater.

It is not enough to allege that your partner took $10,000 out of the company's account without authorization. That conduct might give rise to other claims, but is not conversion unless you can identify the specific units of currency taken. Notwithstanding these challenges, a conversion claim can provide a potent vehicle for the recovery of monetary damages, or the return of the converted property under the right circumstances.

Defamation. Defamation consists of an intentional communication, whether verbal or written, containing false statements about another for the purpose of damaging their reputation. Unfortunately, this sort of trash talk is all too common between business partners who have become upset with each other. To be actionable, the statement cannot be merely an opinion. Instead, it must make a false representation of a tangible fact. Calling someone an asshole is not defamation, but calling him a thief may be. Truth is an absolute defense to a defamation claim.

Usurpation of corporate opportunity. A common issue faced by entrepreneurs is whether they are obligated to pursue new business opportunities presented to them on behalf of the company, or whether they may do so on their own or with others. A corporate opportunity is generally one (a) that falls within the scope of the company's line of business; (b) in which the company has a legitimate business interest or reasonable expectancy; (c) that is of practical advantage to the company; and (d) that the company has the resources to legitimately pursue.

Generally, when a partner is presented with a business opportunity that meets these criteria, the official must first present the opportunity to the company. Only if the company rejects the opportunity can the partner pursue that opportunity for himself, unless otherwise contractually forbidden. If a partner pursues a corporate opportunity for himself without first presenting it to the company, he does so at his peril and may be sued by the company for misappropriation of corporate opportunity and/or for breach of fiduciary duty.

Disputes often arise between companies and their (sometimes former) partners about whether (1) the opportunity was one in which the company had a legitimate expectation or interest; (2) the company has the financial ability to pursue the opportunity; or (3) the official gave the company a meaningful chance to pursue the opportunity before doing so for himself. The more thorough the documentation or other evidence relating to the business opportunity or to the relationships between the parties, the more straightforward the analysis as to whether the opportunity constitutes a corporate opportunity, and the more likely the dispute can be resolved without extensive litigation. Often, this evidence is unavailable or is in conflict with other evidence. In these instances, the murky question of whether the opportunity belongs to the company can become an issue for a jury to decide at trial.

Among the factors that are often persuasive with judges and juries in answering this question are: (a) whether there exists a long-term or exclusive relationship between the company and the individual or entity that constitutes the opportunity; (b) whether the company's organizational documents expressly prohibit or allow corporate officials to engage in business endeavors that compete with the company; (c) whether the company has successfully pursued similar opportunities in the past; (d) whether the official pursued the opportunity openly or surreptitiously; (e) whether the company has the financial resources, manpower, and/or expertise to legitimately pursue the opportunity; and (f) whether the opportunity results from the relationships created while the corporate official was acting on behalf of the company, or whether the official formed the relationships prior to his association with the company.

There are pragmatic issues that must also be considered in connection with asserting or defending a misappropriation of corporate opportunity claims. If the customers or business partners that constitute the business opportunity in dispute learn of the existence of the dispute, they may simply decline to do business with either the company or the officer rather than to become embroiled in the dispute themselves. An old saying about not tossing the baby out with the bathwater comes to mind. Resolving complex disputes concerning the appropriation of business opportunities—by negotiation when possible and by litigation when necessary—requires a delicate balancing act between aggressively pursuing rights of the company or its officers, while simultaneously maintaining the business relationships that constitute the opportunity in dispute.

Misappropriation of trade secrets. If your company profits from information not known to the general public, it may own trade secrets. A trade secret may include patents, a customer or pricing list, a business process, a system or formula, or similar data. If an owner or employee of the company makes use of that trade secret for their own gain, without authorization from the company or consideration back to the company, he or she may well be misappropriating trade secrets.

Data that qualifies as a trade secret is protected under state and federal laws, both of which allow for the award of a money judgment or an injunctive relief, such as a court order precluding use of certain information for financial gain.

CLAIMS FOR EQUITABLE RELIEF

Some courts are empowered to grant equitable relief in addition to, or in place of, awarding money damages.

Declaratory relief. In some instances, courts are permitted to issue declarations as to unsettled issues that will help parties regulate their conduct going forward. Common examples are asking a court to declare whether a restrictive covenant (i.e. non-complete, non-solicit) clause in a contract is enforceable, or who has voting rights or control over a company. Declaratory relief can be a powerful tool in answering questions when partners agree what the contract *says*, but disagree about what it *means*.

Injunctive relief. Certain courts also have the power to issue temporary restraining orders, as well as temporary and/or permanent injunctions. Via injunction, a court orders a person, group, or business either to do or not to do something. For example, a court may order a former employee and his new employer to delete and not use the customer list he downloaded before leaving his old employer. In some instances, a court may appoint a neutral party to serve as its investigator or caretaker in connection with an operating business.

Appointment of auditor or receiver. In some instances, judges have the power to appoint subject matter experts as surrogates. A court may appoint an auditor to scour corporate books to answer a thorny question about where the money went. In extreme situations, she may appoint a receiver to take temporary managerial control of a company and run it until the judge is ready to make a final determination on the merits.

Judicial dissolution. In certain circumstances, a judge is empowered to dissolve a corporate entity. Basically, the court requires that the company's assets be liquidated. Then, the sale proceeds are used to satisfy company debt. Any remaining funds are divided among the shareholders proportionally to their ownership interests. There are two basic patterns that can give rise to a judicial dissolution.

The first is deadlock. A deadlock occurs when no one has authority to act on behalf of the company. Most commonly, this happens when two partners each own fifty percent of the company and one wants to take the company in one direction while the other partner wants to take it in another. Neither holds a majority ownership interest, so neither has control of the company. Absent a legitimate manager, the company is not authorized to take any action.

A second basis for dissolution can occur when the court concludes that the company's management team is engaging in fraud or waste that is bound to lead the company to insolvency.

In many ways, a judicial dissolution is akin to the mutually assured destruction of nuclear war. This is because company assets sold on the courthouse steps pursuant to a judicial dissolution decree are likely to be sold for a fraction of what they are worth. Although a judicial dissolution is rarely a desirable outcome, it can be very effective in breaking a stalemate and forcing a recalcitrant business partner to the negotiating table. If the company's assets are going to be sold one way or another, both partners have incentive to work together to maximize the sale price those assets generate.

PREPARE FOR COURT

Your Case Will Probably Settle

At the inception of a lawsuit, it is easy and tempting to believe that the case will go all the way to trial, and it might. But, it probably won't. More than ninety percent of all civil lawsuits filed in the United States never make it to trial. The vast majority of cases settle somewhere along the way. As Carl von Clausewitz stated, "War is the continuation of politics by other means." Often, litigation, particularly when used to bring resolution of a business dispute, is simply part of the negotiation dance. Offers and counteroffers are exchanged. Tempers flare. Positions solidify, and lawsuits are filed. Discovery is served, depositions taken, six months pass, each litigant pays six months' worth of attorney's invoices. Then they revisit the wisdom of a fight to the death.

The additional insights into the risks and rewards of litigation are fleshed out through discovery and trial preparation. All of these factors work together to de-solidify the positions that hardened when the dispute was fresh and new. At this point, many litigants revisit their settlement dialogue and find a way to resolve their dispute.

Expect Delays

Litigation is time consuming. It is not uncommon in many jurisdictions for a case to take years from inception to trial. Appeals can take additional years. The vast majority of cases settle, but those that don't are in for a long journey.

It's Going to Get Expensive

Lawsuits are expensive. Hourly rates for an experienced business lawyer can range between $250 to $750 depending on experience, market, and other factors. Further, most lawyers will insist on a substantial retainer upfront that she will bill against at her hourly rate. This is because once she enters an appearance in a pending lawsuit, she is your lawyer, and obligated to represent you zealously, whether she is getting paid or not. To withdraw from representation of a client in a pending lawsuit, the lawyer must get permission from the judge. Given this, most lawyers will hedge their bets and insist on a retainer up front that will cover at least the initial phases of the litigation. The more obnoxious your partner (or his lawyer) is, the more work your lawyer will have to do. Those hours can add up quickly.

Lawsuits Are Public Records

If you sue your business partner, or she sues you, the court filings of that lawsuit will be in the public record. In some jurisdictions, these filings are available online for all to see. Do you really want your customers, lenders, vendors, and competitors sifting through your dirty laundry?

Often, in cases involving the violation of non-compete or non-solicit clauses, the usurpation of corporate opportunities, the misappropriation of trade secrets, or defamation, a business's customers are the key witnesses. There is little you can do that will drive your customers to a competitor faster than for you or your partner to subpoena them to a deposition or to force them to testify at trial. Winning your case can mean losing your best business relationships. Are you prepared to accept that risk?

Once You File a Lawsuit, You May Not Be Able to Stop It

If your dispute with your business partner becomes sufficiently intractable that one of you sues the other, it's a safe bet that the other is going to assert counterclaims against the one who initiated the lawsuit in the first place. There are several reasons for this.

First, there is very likely a frustration—legitimate or otherwise—going both ways between the parties. Reasonable people can disagree. You believe your partner breached the operating agreement by failing to follow up on new opportunities. Yet, he believes you are breaching your fiduciary duties to the company by insisting that it chase proverbial windmills. Sometimes it's just a matter of perspective.

Second, a good offense makes a great defense. If it's only the plaintiff asserting claims against the defendant, the plaintiff holds all the cards. The issues presented for resolution by the court are, by and large, the issues the plaintiff wants to talk about. Invariably, these issues are what the defendant did wrong and how the plaintiff was injured. Further, if the plaintiff is the only party pursuing relief, that plaintiff can generally stop the case at any time by dismissing it.

However, if the defendant asserts a counterclaim against the plaintiff, the dynamic changes. Now, the issues before the court are not just if and what the defendant did wrong, but what the plaintiff did as well. Similarly, the plaintiff no longer has the luxury of dismissing the lawsuit and making it go away if and when it becomes inconvenient. Even if the plaintiff were to dismiss, the defendant's counterclaims would still remain pending and the plaintiff would still have to defend herself from those counterclaims.

Many times, an entrepreneur, frustrated with his business partner's actions, will file suit with the expectation that the partner will react defensively, become intimidated, and settle quickly. They are often surprised to learn that their partner harbors similar frustrations with them, and vents those frustrations in the form of an aggressive and well-coordinated counter attack. What the entrepreneur thought would be a surgical strike erodes into messy and protracted litigation that feels like a bloodbath. Anticipate this possibility and account for it in your preparations.

Make Sure What You're Fighting About is Worth Fighting For

Litigation is expensive, time consuming, and stressful. It can wear on your soul. Before you subject yourself to the process, make sure it's worth it for your financial, physical, and mental wellness.

There is another reason to be circumspect about the battles you fight. Think about it from the judge's perspective. All day long, every day, for years, people come in front of him with disagreements that they have not been able to solve by themselves. Some are big and legitimate. Some are small and petty. When the judge brings resolution to the larger, legitimate issues, he feels good about what he does. When he presides over smaller, less important matters, he can feel like he's helping children learn to share the same toy. It can be exhausting.

If you engage in petty power plays, you can expect to be called before the judge to explain your conduct. If the judge gets frustrated with you on the little things, it becomes harder for the judge to see things your way when it comes to the big things. For this reason, every time you are in front of the judge, you want to be the one wearing the white hat. Anything you do that tarnishes the hat reflects poorly on you. Keep your hat white and your conduct clean.

CHAPTER 6

12 Common Questions Clients Ask When Going Through a Business Divorce . . . and the Answers

This chapter is dedicated to answering the twelve most common questions that come up from business owners stuck in an intractable dispute with a business partner.

1. What if I can't access the company's books and records?
2. What if my business partner and I never signed a partnership agreement?

3. Can I kick my partner out of the business? Can she kick me out?
4. Can I start a competing business? Can my partner?
5. I/my business partner put money into the company, but I don't know if it was a loan or an equity contribution. How do I figure it out? Does it matter?
6. Can I sue my partner for ruining the business?
7. Can I have my partner arrested for stealing from me/the business?
8. I don't want to be defensive or reactionary. How do I take the offensive?
9. Most of the company's clients are my friends. Their contact information is in my phone. That data belongs to me, right?
10. What is the difference between a direct claim and a derivative claim?
11. Can I make my business partner pay my attorney's fees if we go to court?
12. I/my company just got served with a subpoena or a summons. It's total B.S. Can I ignore it?

THE ANSWERS

1. What if I can't access to the company's books and records?

Maybe your business partner was tasked with maintaining the company's minute book. Or, maybe she was the organized one. Or, you moved. Perhaps your computer crashed. Perhaps your partner has effectively frozen you out of the operations of the business and you have very little access to information. Maybe you are the one with all the records and your partner is the one wondering what's going on.

I once represented a financial advisor whom we'll call Joe. Joe was employed by and owned a minority interest in a wealth planning firm that we'll call The Volcano. Joe was not involved in the company's management. He knew that The Volcano did well, but did not know much about its balance sheet or how much his co-owners made. A management shakeup left Joe concerned about The Volcano's culture, as well as its long-term prospects. Joe also suspected that certain managers might have their hands in the company's cookie jar.

Rather than endure what was becoming a toxic work environment, Joe resigned and offered to both cooperate in a smooth transition and to sell his ownership interest back at a fair price. The Volcano erupted, rejecting his offer and spewing unsubstantiated allegations that Joe had stolen its trade secrets and clients.

Joe kept his cool. With my help, he politely and persistently asserted his right as an owner to review The Volcano's financial records. Was management taking more than that to which they were entitled? We'll never know. Rather than comply with Joe's request for information, The Volcano's management team agreed to buy back Joe's ownership interest at a reasonable price and Joe was able to move on.

Don't underestimate the power of an owner's right to review the company's books and records, particularly in situations where that information has historically been hard to come by. All too often, majority owners and those in management roles use their position to intimidate, bully, or ignore minority owners into complacency. First, the annual shareholders meeting gets postponed. Then, it never gets rescheduled. Then, the financials are sent out a few months later than in prior years. Then, they don't get sent out at all. Although this is all too common, it is not acceptable.

If you are a minority owner of a business and any of this sounds familiar, it is time to assert your rights and insist on looking behind the curtain. If you are the company manager who has been thwarting the efforts of another owner to gain access to information concerning the business, just know that doing so may subject the company, and potentially you, to liability or other legal sanction.

Most states require business entities, whether they be corporations, limited liability companies, partnerships, or otherwise, to maintain in a central location specific business records, and to make certain those records are available to the owners of the business on written request. These business records can be divided into the following three categories:

> **Organizational records.** Organizational records are those that reveal the type of legal entity that the business is, as well as the identity and voting rights of its owners and management. By-laws, articles of incorporation or organization, operating agreements, shareholder agreements, and partnership agreements generally fall into this category as would meeting minutes, resolutions, and any amendments to operating agreements or by-laws.

Transactional records. Transactional records are those which relate to the entity's business activities and relationships with third parties. This might include the entity's office space lease, its vendor and customer contracts, and titles to real estate or equipment.

Financial records. Financial and accounting records are those which reflect the financial affairs of the entity, including tax returns, balance sheets, profit and loss statements, bank statements, and other documents demonstrating the financial condition of the business.

As an owner, the extent of your rights of inspection and the amount of information the company is obligated to disclose to you, can vary depending on whether the company is a corporation, a limited liability company (LLC), a general partnership, or a limited partnership. The right of inspection can also vary if you have previously agreed upon access rights or limitations. In some instances, the right to review is unrestricted. In others, the owner making the request must identify the legitimate business purpose for which he is requesting the information. Similarly, what an owner can do with the information on receipt may be restricted. For example, you as an owner may have the right to know who the company's customers and vendors are and how much they are paying or being paid, but be precluded from using that information to start a competing business.

The right to inspect these records is qualified and not absolute. Requesting to view the records does not give you unfettered access to any corporate records simply by virtue of having an ownership interest in the corporation. In some instances, you must articulate a proper purpose for your request. Essentially, the broader your request and the greater access sought, the more particular the shareholder must be in identifying the purpose for the request.

Typically, it is best to make this request in a formal letter. Better still, hire a lawyer to send it. Fair or not, law firm letterhead often results in a more thorough response. If, after exercising your statutory and/or contractual right to review the books and records of the company, the company still refuses to cooperate, many states have laws that allow you to file suit to compel access to the company's books and records, and for an expedited hearing to be held on that request.

If the court finds your records request reasonable, and the company's response unreasonable, the court has the power not only to compel the production of the records, but also to require the company (or potentially its managers) to pay your attorney's fees incurred in bringing suit. In an effort to balance the interests of the corporation with this disclosure, the court may also impose reasonable restrictions on your use or distribution of the corporate records, as the circumstances may warrant.

It is worth restating that if you don't have unfettered access to the organizational, transactional, and financial records of a business that you own a piece of, it's time to take action to gain that access. Whatever is going on behind the curtain is not helping you.

2. What if my business partner and I never signed a partnership agreement?

When people think of contracts, they often think of formal, written documents and fine print. But, many business transactions, large and small, are discussed and agreed upon verbally. Rather than affixing signatures to a formal document, a hand shake is all that memorializes the deal. When each party performs as the other expects, people appreciate the lack of formality and enjoy the trust that they share in one another.

In the excitement and goodwill associated with starting the business or bringing on a partner, owners often never get around to a written partnership agreement. If you find yourself there, you're not alone. Most states have laws that impose default rules that govern the relationships between partners in a partnership, shareholders in a corporation, or members in a limited liability company to the extent that a written agreement signed by the owners does not address the issue at hand.

Some of these default rules may surprise you. For example, in some states, if the owners of an LLC have no operating agreement, each is entitled to an equal vote and an equal share of the profits, regardless how much or how little of the company they each may own. In these instances, those holding a small minority interest suddenly find themselves much more in power than they previously believed.

3. Can I kick my partner out of the business? Can she kick me out?

A common misconception held by many entrepreneurs is that their ownership interests in a business entity can simply be revoked by the business or taken by other owners. Generally, an ownership interest in a business entity cannot be so easily lost.

Disputes between and among the various owners of a business often arise because one believes that another is not doing enough to contribute to the success of the business. As a result, one owner (often with a controlling interest) will attempt to revoke, take, or simply ignore the ownership interests of others with whom he disagrees. Often, a call is made to the company's CPA or bookkeeper with instructions that one owner's interest in the business is to be deleted from the corporate records, or perhaps transferred to another owner. The disfavored (and unsuspecting) owner often first learns of his purported divesture when he receives a final K-1 from the accountant the following year.

Yet, without some pre-agreed upon procedure, an ownership interest in a business entity generally cannot be forfeited. Instead, once a business interest is granted, it generally cannot be revoked.

The dissolution of a partnership can involve acrimonious circumstances and can occur abruptly. It is not uncommon for one partner to try to gain an advantage during this process. Even when two partners have resolved to end their partnership, the law demands that they continue to act in the utmost good faith until the business is wound up, and affords a remedy for a breach of that standard.

There are ways to minimize a partner's involvement in the business without violating his rights. Sometimes this is referred to as a freeze-out. And, as with temperature, whether the conduct is appropriate or not is generally a matter of degree. A common method of freeze-out is where a controlling shareholder who is active in the business fires the minority shareholder and then votes to pay himself a salary that consumes profits that would otherwise be available to other owners by distribution. If the salary is market rate, or slightly higher, that decision will likely be insulated by the business judgment rule.

However, if the controlling shareholders' salary is three times market rate, that conduct will be much harder to justify if challenged in court and the perpetrator of that action may be liable for breaching fiduciary duties.

4. Can I start a competing business? Can my business partner?

It depends. If you or your business partner has an enforceable restrictive covenant in a shareholder agreement, employment agreement, or similar document that precludes competition or solicitation, then you engage in a competitive behavior at your peril. Whether a restrictive covenant, such as a non-compete, non-solicitation, or non-recruitment provision is enforceable can vary widely depending on what state you live in. Generally, the more restrictive the covenant, the greater the chance that it may be unenforceable.

Alternatively, if your shareholder agreement expressly allows owners to participate in competing ventures, then you may do so. If no document addresses the issue, the answer generally depends on your role with the business. If you have a say in management, competing with your business could be problematic. If your role is as a passive investor, you have much more freedom to engage in a competing venture. Even then, you must be careful not to use information or resources that belong to the company to advance your competitive activity. If you do, or if your partner did, you or he may be subject to liability. Get a lawyer to help you figure it out.

5. I/my business partner put money into the company, but I don't know if it was a loan or an equity contribution. How do I figure it out? Does it matter?

A common area of dispute between business co-owners is the characterization of their respective capital contributions as either the purchase of equity in the enterprise or a loan to it. Often, the pressing circumstances driving the business's need for the capital can distract those involved from thinking through, agreeing to, or properly documenting the nature of the transaction. The passage of time rarely clarifies the confusion.

As time passes, and circumstances change, so too can memories. The company's financial performance often dictates the differing recollections of the transaction by the company and the investor. If the business is doing well, the investor is more likely to claim an ownership interest and the corresponding right to share in profits. Yet, the company is more likely to treat the investor as a creditor, entitled to a return of principal and interest, but no more. If the company is just treading water, it is more likely to claim the investor as an owner, pointing to the lack of profits as justification for refusing to pay distributions. But, the investor is more likely to claim creditor status, demanding the return of investment, with interest. Because the respective rights of the company and the investor will vary greatly depending on how the transaction is characterized, the stakes are high.

When faced with these questions, courts look to a variety of factors to determine whether a contribution should be considered an equity purchase or a loan. Generally, a loan is the delivery by one party to, and the receipt by another party of, a sum of money upon an agreement—expressed or implied—to repay the principal with or without interest. Alternatively, an equity contribution is the investment of money or something else of value in pursuit of profits, often from the efforts of others.

In absence of clear documentation—such as a promissory note evidencing a loan, or a stock purchase agreement evidencing an ownership interest—courts generally look to the conduct of the parties to determine whether there was an implied agreement to repay a loan or to purchase an ownership interest. This can be a notation on the memo line of a check, or a detailed email. The manner in which the parties characterize the transaction in accounting records or tax returns can be telling. Was a K-1 issued? Is the contribution treated as a liability on the company's balance sheet? Did the company make payments to the investor contemporaneously with distributions to other owners, or did it make consistent (interest only) payments, regardless of profitability? Any of these factors may be determinative.

6. Can I sue my partner for ruining the business?

It depends. If your partner breached a contract of fiduciary duty, misappropriated trade secrets, or usurped corporate opportunities, then yes. See Chapter 5 for more on these claims. Alternatively, if your partner tried to act in the best interests of the business, but is just a bad businessman, then no. His ineptitude will be protected by the business judgment rule. That rule, discussed previously, is a policy of judicial restraint born on the recognition that corporate officers and managers are generally more qualified to make business decisions than are judges and juries. If a business decision was made in good faith based on a reasonable analysis, it will not be second guessed by the courts. The presumption of reasonable business judgment can be overcome when there is evidence of self-dealing. In other words, if a manager hires his wife's company to clean the office and pays four times the going rate, that decision will not be protected by the business judgment rule.

7. Can I have my partner arrested for stealing from me/the business?

Generally, it's not a good idea. The following story illustrates why. Jack, Janet, and Chrissy each own one third of, and are employed by, an LLC that operates a successful business. Jack and Janet tire of Chrissy and undertake to freeze her out of the business. Either out of spite or in an attempt to create leverage, Jack takes a computer necessary for the day-to-day operations of the business and hides it away. Chrissy promptly emails Jack to tell him that he's fired. Chrissy then calls a friend at the local police department and reports that a former employee stole a company laptop.

The police go to Jack's house to confront him. Jack admits to taking the computer and the police arrest him. Jack spends the weekend in jail. On Monday morning, a prosecutor looks at the file and determines that the laptop belongs to a company of which the accused owns 33 percent. Based on this, the prosecutor concludes that the dispute is of a civil nature rather than a criminal matter and drops the charges. Jack hires a lawyer and sues

Chrissy for malicious prosecution, false arrest, and false imprisonment.

Several years ago, I represented the Chrissy in this story. The case went all the way to a jury trial. Chrissy "won", but only after spending two years in litigation, and tens of thousands of dollars on her defense.

That experience informs my skepticism of the utility of involving law enforcement in a business dispute. In the vast majority of situations, you would do well not to do so. Below are some factors to consider before getting law enforcement involved in a business dispute:

> **Law enforcement generally stays out of civil matters.** If the police or a prosecutor gets a sense that there is an existing business relationship between the accuser and the accused, and the dispute does not involve violence, they are unlikely to get or stay involved.
>
> **Calling the police might get you sued.** If charges are dropped, or the accused is acquitted, he or she may have a claim against you for false arrest, false imprisonment, or malicious prosecution. Even if you had a good faith basis on which to press criminal charges and are ultimately successful in defending the civil claim, you will pay for it in time, money, and aggravation.
>
> **Just because you're the one who calls the police does not necessarily mean that you won't be the one who leaves in handcuffs.** The police will conduct their own investigation and may be skeptical of your story. Don't be surprised if your business partner tells the

authorities some nasty things about you, whether true or not. After all, his liberty is on the line. Depending on who the police believe, you may be the one who ends up arrested.

You have no control over the criminal process. You will have little to no say in the scope or duration of a criminal investigation. Information generally flows one way in these matters, and that's toward law enforcement. You may have little idea about the status of the investigation for months or even longer.

Information or property you need to run your business, or to pursue civil claims against your business partner could be impounded as evidence. In criminal prosecutions, it is important for law enforcement to demonstrate a "chain of custody" for evidence. This insulates them from criticism by the defense that evidence is somehow tainted. Police often impound the items in an evidence locker, sometimes for months or even years. Your need for an item to run your business will take a back seat to law enforcement's interest in preserving the chain of custody.

If you threaten criminal prosecution in an attempt to strengthen your negotiating position, you could be prosecuted for extortion. You don't want that. Don't do it.

There are many good reasons not to involve law enforcement in a business dispute. This is not to say you should never do so. If your business partner inflicts or threatens violence on you or anyone else, dial 911. If your business partner is defrauding customers, lenders, or the government, notify the authorities. But, if you or your business is the primary victim of your business partner's conduct, you may be best served by talking to a lawyer about your civil remedies before you call the police.

8. I don't want to be defensive or reactionary. How do I take the offensive?

I get this question a lot. Clients come to me seeking help in resolving a dispute with their business partner. We talk about options and potential outcomes. I give them homework. It may be creating a timeline, gathering and returning information, confirming that there is no company data stored on their personal devices, or producing documents. The response I get often is: "This is all the stuff my partner wants from me. Who cares what he wants? When are we going to go after what I want?" The answer is, when the time is right. But that time may not be now.

Those who live in glass houses shouldn't throw stones. It's easy to think of the demand letters or discovery you or your lawyer sends as reasonable and necessary, but view the letters or discovery you receive from your former business partner-turned adversary as litigious and harassing. Sometimes it is, but more likely, it's just your perspective. It might feel good today to tell your former partner and his lawyer to pound sand and then ignore their requests for information. However, you will come to regret it in the long run. Judges do not appreciate litigants or lawyers who shirk the rules, antagonize each other, or unnecessarily expand the litigation. Indeed, certain behavior could cause a jury to make you pay your business partner's attorney's fees. Be strategic, and don't let your anger dictate your actions.

Think about it from a judge's perspective for a moment. The same day she hears your case, she may convict a pedophile, hear testimony related to a catastrophic injury, or see the same opioid addict back in her courtroom for the third time this year. The world is full of people who need the adult supervision that only a judge can offer. When a judge gets a business case, she is hopeful and expects that she will have two (or more) reasonable, competent people, who have a dispute, and who seek the court's assistance in resolving that dispute in a sensible and professional manner. If the judge gets the sense that for all your success in the business world, you need just as much babysitting as parole violators and drug addicts, you are not likely to get much sympathy.

You can take control, but be smart about it. Get and keep your own house in order so your partner doesn't have an easy target at which to take aim. By keeping your affairs in order, maintaining distinctions between personal and corporate property, and following the law and rules of the court, you demonstrate credibility, both to your partner and to any judge or jury who may ultimately be called upon to resolve your business dispute.

9. Most of the company's clients are my friends. Their contact information is in my phone. That data belongs to me, right?

There are a myriad of personal electronic devices on which to store information and communicate. Who owns those devices and the data on them can have critical implications when business co-owners battle to control the company, to join another, or to leave and start a competing one.

Companies generally fall into two categories with respect to electronic devices used for business purposes. The first is BYOD—often referred to as "Bring Your Own Device". The second is COPE—"Company-Owned, Personally Enabled" devices. Your business may already have formal policies (probably designed for employees) that speak to who owns the device. If so, it's a fair bet that the same policy applies to you, and you would do well to follow it. You can probably also hold your co-owners to it. If there is no formal policy, the question is less clear.

Factors to consider in making this determination are:

- Who owns the device? If the company owns the device (or reimburses you for its cost) it may also own the data on it.
- Who paid for the device? The entity that pays for the monthly service is likely to be viewed as the entity that owns the device.
- How were the contacts generated? Did you bring these contacts to the company from prior relationships, or did you develop the relationships by taking these folks to lunch with the company credit card?
- Is the contact information backed up on/to a company computer, server, or cloud account? If so, the company may own the data.

These inquiries can be distilled into a general principal: The more the company funded or supplied resources in the creation, development, storage, or maintenance of the data, the more likely the data belongs to the company. Copying this data, or using it for purposes competitive with the company, can subject you to liability either to the company or to its other owners. So, be careful of your conduct, and keep a close eye on your partner's use of this data as well.

If you suspect that your business partner or an employee may have helped himself to the company's data, consider hiring a computer forensics expert to take a deep dive into the company's network. A good technician can quickly identify what data was downloaded, by whom, and when, based on a scan of the network. Your partner may have a perfectly legitimate reason for emailing the company's customer list to his personal email address one day before offering to sell you his ownership interest in the company, but wouldn't you like to know what his reason is before you negotiate with him?

10. What is the difference between a direct claim and a derivative claim?

A common issue that arises in disputes between and among co-owners of a business is whether the claims of an aggrieved owner are "direct" or "derivative". The distinction is important for both procedural and substantive reasons. At its most basic, direct claims are based on legal rights that belong to the individual co-owner, who can bring a claim in court in his own name to vindicate his rights. In a derivative action, that same co-owner (whether corporation shareholder or LLC member) brings a derivative claim on behalf of the entity to vindicate a harm suffered by the entity as a whole. Derivative claims are often necessary where the owner seeking to bring the claim owns a non-controlling interest in the entity.

The risks of being a minority shareholder in a corporation (or member of an LLC) are well known. Without a controlling interest in the company, a minority owner often has little say in how the company is run. So long as management acts in the best interests of the company, it will be insulted from liability by the business judgment rule. But, what happens when management abuses its authority, using the company's resources for personal gain, or steering corporate opportunities away from the company and toward management's other business interests?

In these instances, management subjects itself to liability for breach of fiduciary duty. But, to whom is management liable—the aggrieved owner or the company itself? The answer, like that to so many legal questions, is that it depends.

Management's fiduciary duties run to the company and its owners. If those duties are breached, it is generally the company that suffers the direct harm, and the company that has the right to bring suit to recover resulting damages. But, given its control of the company, it's a safe bet that management is not going to cause the company to pursue a lawsuit back against management. What's an aggrieved owner to do?

In most instances, the remedy may be to bring a derivative action in which the minority owner brings suit in the name, and on behalf, of the company and against the company's management. Any ultimate recovery is received by the company, such that the company benefits directly, and all of its owners benefit indirectly in the form of increased company value.

As with most things in life and the law, there is an exception to the derivative claim requirement. In limited instances, where the minority owner can show that he suffered a "special injury" that is distinct from that suffered by the company or its other owners, he may bring a direct claim and keep any recovery for himself. For example, if management caused the company to make distributions to all but one owner, that owner would suffer a harm not experienced by the company or the other members, for which he may recover.

There are procedural nuances and strategic considerations to noticing and asserting derivative claims. A good lawyer can help you sort them out. At its core, the determination as to whether a claim against company management should be brought directly or derivatively hinges on whether the company or its owner was most directly harmed by the conduct alleged.

11. Can I make my business partner pay my attorney's fees if we go to court?

Deciding whether to pursue litigation to resolve a dispute is a business decision. The associated expense is one of many factors to consider. The default rule, known as the "American Rule", is that each party pays its own attorney's fees in court, win or lose. The rationale behind this rule is that fear of the possibility of having to pay an adversary's attorney's fees should not discourage a party from seeking redress in court. This can frustrate business owners, who often believe that the costs associated with getting justice should be borne by the party who caused the problem. Fortunately, there are two broad exceptions to the American Rule that find frequent application in business litigation.

Prevailing party provision. Many contracts provide that if a dispute is resolved in court, the winner—or prevailing party—can recover attorney's fees from the losing party. Prevailing party attorney's fees provisions are routinely enforced by courts and can be a powerful tool in facilitating settlement discussions out of court or recouping litigation costs in it.

Bad faith. The second broad exception to the American Rule applies where one party acts in "bad faith" or is "stubbornly litigious". Although virtually every litigant believes that his adversary acted capriciously, courts take a narrower view. To constitute bad faith, the offending conduct must generally (1) cause the prevailing party unnecessary trouble and expense; or (2) be in direct contravention of established facts or law. These can be subjective standards to be sure. What appears frivolous to some can be interpreted as a *bona fide* dispute to others.

To increase the likelihood of recovering attorney's fees in court, you would do well to wear the white hat and document improper conduct.

Wear the white hat. By upholding your end of a business relationship, treating others fairly, and compromising to bring closure to disputes as they arise, you demonstrate your own good faith. In addition to reducing significant business disputes in the first place, you win the hearts and minds of judges and juries, thereby increasing the likelihood of a favorable attorney's fees award.

> **Document improper conduct.** Finding an adversary's email promising one thing, and a second email written six months later disavowing the commitment can go a long way to demonstrating the adversary's bad faith. Save emails, invoices, contracts, and other deal-related information. You never know when you will may need them.

Incurring attorney's fees in court is a given. *Recovering* them from an adversary is not. You should not undertake litigation expecting your attorney's fees to be paid by your adversary; however, following the steps above will greatly increase the chances of that outcome.

12. I/my company just got served with a subpoena or a summons. It's total B.S. Can I ignore it?

You shouldn't. A subpoena is a command either to show up in court to testify or to bring documents, or to sit for a deposition. Ignoring it could get you or your company held in contempt of court and sanctioned financially. In extreme situations, you could be incarcerated, if only briefly. You don't want any of these things.

A summons is the formal document that accompanies a new lawsuit (typically called a complaint or a petition) when it is served on a defendant. This service of process, as it is known, is generally accomplished by a deputy sheriff, marshal, or private process server hand delivering the complaint and an accompanying summons to the defendant. Some states allow service of process by certified mail.

In the case of an individual defendant, the process server will generally knock on the front door of their home or show up at their office to serve the complaint. In the case of an entity, the complaint may be served on a corporate officer, manager, or the company's registered agent. The company's registered agent is the person on file with the Secretary of State in the state in which the entity was organized, and is authorized to accept service of process on behalf of the entity.

Most lawsuits are served personally on the defendant, but there are alternatives. For example, a complaint may be served on an individual defendant by delivering it to a family member who is of "suitable age and discretion" at the individual's home. Although this is a case-by-case inquiry, a spouse likely qualifies; a minor child likely does not. If, after reasonable attempts to locate an individual defendant, he cannot be found, a judge may authorize the defendant to be served by publication. Basically, the plaintiff runs a notice for four weeks in the official legal organ (often a newspaper) of the county in which the defendant resides, alerting the defendant of the pending lawsuit. Similarly, if a corporate officer, manager, or registered agent cannot be found, an entity can be served by delivering the complaint to the Secretary of State with which the entity is registered, and sending a copy of the complaint to the company's address on file by registered mail.

Once served, a defendant generally has between a week and thirty days, depending on the jurisdiction, in which to file an "answer". Basically, an answer consists of a point-by-point response to the individually numbered paragraphs of the complaint, either admitting or denying each allegation. If an answer is not filed timely, the allegations of the complaint are deemed admitted and the defendant is considered to be in default. Once in default, the defendant loses the opportunity to contest those allegations of the complaint deemed admitted. Entry of a default judgment typically follows. Once a judgment is entered, the plaintiff can undertake to collect on the judgment with the help of the deputy sheriff by selling the defendant's assets on the courthouse steps or by draining funds directly from the defendant's bank account. Far too many defendants find themselves on the wrong end of a default judgment because they did not act quickly when served with a complaint, or because they did not even realize that they had been served. Don't be one of them.

Getting sued is never fun, but losing before you even get started is even worse. There are steps you can take to minimize the possibility of a default judgment or other sanctions being entered against you or your company.

If you are served, or wonder if you were, talk to a lawyer immediately. If applicable, notify your insurance carrier or broker as well. Do not assume that if you have turned the complaint over to your insurance carrier that the complaint is off your plate. Often, insurance companies deliberate (delay) long beyond the time to answer before even making a coverage decision. By then, it can be too late.

CHAPTER 7

Moving On—With or Without a Business Partner

Ending a business relationship can be taxing, stressful, and expensive. But, it can also be liberating. You become unshackled from the burdens of a lousy business partner. Where will you go from here? Perhaps you already know. If so, great! If not, take some time and figure it out. Maybe you want to be in a new industry. Maybe you're not so sure you want to own your own business again, or at least not right away. Give yourself time and the permission to ruminate. Do not rush into another business partnership. This is not to say you should never take on another business partner, as they can bring enormous value to the table. Just give yourself the space to figure out what went wrong with the last one.

The bright side of having been through the messy business breakup that caused you to read this far into a book titled *Life's Too Short for a Bad Business Partner* is that you now have experience with some of the warning signs of an unproductive business relationship. This experience is also likely to strengthen your resolve to more thoroughly vet any prospective partner in the future.

Just because someone was a fun college roommate or even a good colleague at work does not mean you should trust him with your financial future. Consider performing a background check on your prospective partner, and offer to share the results of one performed on you. Exchange personal financial statements and credit reports. If your prospective partner has a bankruptcy in his past, you want to know that before it is time to qualify for a loan or other funding. These are sensitive topics. All the more reason to have the discussion on the front end. If, after an initial dialogue or exchange of information, your "Spidey senses" are tingling, listen closely and dig deeper.

Download a comprehensive list of the types of questions you could ask and information you could request in your due diligence of a prospective business partner at www.williampiercy.com/resources.

When you are satisfied that there are no closet skeletons to fear, have an in-depth discussion with your partner about objectives, expectations, money, operations, and exit strategies. Too many partnerships begin without thinking through these key issues. Discussing and negotiating the nuts and bolts of the relationship will offer a glimpse of what being in business with your new partner will be like.

Objectives and Expectations

- Does your partner view the enterprise as an "all-in" 80-hour-per-week operation, or a lifestyle company that will allow more time for family and travel?
- Does he envision a long-term commitment, or does he want to sell out in three years?
- What sort of income does he reasonably expect to achieve?

Money Issues

- Will each partner make an initial contribution to start the company? If so, should any portion of that contribution be treated as a loan, or will it all be a capital contribution?
- If the company gets into a financial bind, what are the obligations of partners to put in additional capital?
- How will partners be compensated? Will each draw a salary? If times are tough, will that salary be deferred?

Operational Issues

- Is a certain partner going to be in charge of day-to-day operations? What are the limits on the authority of the partner in charge of day-to-day operations?
- Will there be a division of responsibilities and labor between the partners?
- How much of a time commitment is expected of each partner?

Legal Issues

- What are the partners' "duty of loyalty" expectations. Can a partner work for, or be involved with, a competitive company?

- How will the partners resolve issues of deadlock?
- Are there restrictive covenants you want to impose on the partners?
- If the business is successful, at what point do you want to sell? If it is not profitable, at what point do you pull the plug?

Exit Strategy

- What are the partners' respective exit strategies?
- Will you have the right to force a buyout if you want out? How will that work?

Once you find common ground on these issues, have your agreement written up by an experienced business lawyer who will work only for you. This will prevent any conflict of interest issues that might inhibit a lawyer from giving you candid advice. When you are comfortable with the agreement, sign it and make sure your partner does so too. Keep your copy! By working through these issues on the front end and memorializing that agreement, you maximize the opportunity for a successful business partnership.

Final Thoughts

Whether you are unsure about your business relationship and looking to repair it, or you are ready to kick your partner to the curb, you now have the tools to get where you want to go. Take a deep breath and accept that something must change. Then, make that change happen, before change happens to you. Gather your information. Assemble your team. Prepare for a change. Have a candid conversation with your business partner. Negotiate fairly, and from a position of strength. Be prepared to walk away if you can, or to fight if you cannot. Focus on the future. And thrive.

ABOUT THE AUTHOR

Healthy business relationships are an essential component of business success. When disputes cause business relationships to sour, declining productivity and revenues are sure to follow. William Piercy works with business owners to bring successful and efficient resolution to a wide variety of business disputes.

Based on his two decades of practice in the "corporate divorce" arena, William understands the challenges that can arise from internal dissension within the management, operations, and ownership of a closely held business. Through hard work, candid advice, and effective advocacy, William helps clients end bad business relationships so they can move forward with better ones.

William earned his undergraduate degree from the University of Florida in 1994, and his law degree from Emory University School of Law in 1997. William was named a Georgia "Super Lawyer" in the area of business litigation in 2012 and has been so named in every year since. Previously, William was a Super Lawyers "Rising Star" (2011-2009, 2006). *Georgia Trend* magazine recognized William as being among the state's 2018 Legal Elite, as selected by his peers. William also received a Martindale-Hubble AV Preeminent rating based on peer review for legal ability and ethical standards. William is an Eagle Scout.

ACKNOWLEDGMENTS

Writing a book, even a short one, is hard. And lonely. And time consuming. I could not have finished this work without the support of my beautiful wife Dawn, and the inspiration of my amazing son Mitchell. Thank you both for being a part of my life.

I also want to thank all the boots on the ground who made this project possible. Anita Henderson, my coach at www.writeyourlife.net, brought enthusiasm, experience, and an occasional kick in the pants to this effort. I owe an enormous debt of gratitude to my beta readers: Amanda Hammett, Gary Heege, John Lenz, Katherine Stuckey, and Jessica Wood. Their insights helped me tighten my focus on you, the reader. For the illustrations throughout this work, I have my good friend, Chris Frishe, at www.graphictechnique.com to thank. Chris and I have known each other since we were in elementary school together. On any given day, it's a fair bet that at least one of us was doodling on the back of math worksheets in class. He has a knack for it. I do not. Thank you, Chris, for sharing your talent.

Finally, I thank my friends and colleagues at my law firm, Berman Fink Van Horn P.C. The opportunity to practice law with smart, ethical lawyers who don't take themselves too seriously is a blessing for which I am thankful every day.